A TREASURY OF MIRACLES FOR TEENS

True Stories of God's Presence Today

Karen Kingsbury

Faith Words

New York Boston Nashville

FaithWords
Hachette Book Group
1290 Avenue of the Americas
New York, NY 10104

www.faithwords.com

Printed in the United States of America

RRD-C

Originally published in hardcover by Hachette Book Group.
First trade edition: April 2015

10 9 8 7 6 5 4 3 2 1

FaithWords is a division of Hachette Book Group, Inc.
The FaithWords name and logo are trademarks of Hachette Book Group, Inc.

LCCN: 2002117138

ISBN: 978-1-4555-5886-5 (pbk.)

Dedicated to

Donald, my prince charming. You are my dream come true, the one I lean on and look to. I love you always and forever. Also to Kelsey, Tyler, Austin, EJ, Sean, and Joshua . . . the lyrics of my song. And to God Almighty, the greatest Author of all, who has—for now—blessed me with these.

Introduction

It's easy to look at life and wonder what it's all about. Especially if you're just starting the journey into adulthood. You've watched terrorists attack the United States, and stood by in horror while the tragedy at Columbine High School captured the nation's attention. It would be easy to feel nervous about everything from the classmate sitting beside you in Algebra to our national security. In fact, you could watch TV or read the newspaper and get discouraged, start thinking that God isn't around anymore. Or that somehow he doesn't care.

That's where this book comes in.

Over the last few years I've heard from hundreds of teens like you—guys and girls who've read my novels and decided to share their amazing stories with me. Some of them involve mysterious people who just might've been angels. Other stories show God's miraculous hand at work in a dozen other ways.

But the point is God does care about you. He knows you're walking through the minefield of adolescence and He has a message for you: you're not alone. If you're the lonely girl sitting by yourself at lunchtime, God's beside you. The popular jock with a public smile and a private fear? He's waiting for you to trust him. If you're lonely, afraid, or even a little concerned about tomorrow, God wants you to rest easy. He has a plan for each of you, for every one of your todays and tomorrows.

And not just any old plan. A good plan, a great plan.

Okay, it's time to get started. Find a quiet place in your room or call up a friend you can read aloud with, and take a deep breath. The book you're holding is a treasure chest, and the stories within it are a series of precious jewels. Each written and shared with you here to remind you of the greatest truth of all.

God loves you.

Now that you understand a little more about the stories you'll be reading, buckle your seatbelts and get ready to do some treasure-hunting. The experience might just change your life forever.

The Miracle of Love

For Tanner Woods, that summer should have been the best ever. He was fifteen, tall and handsome, a standout football player at Thousand Oaks High School in Southern California. He was also an excellent student. Come fall, Tanner would have a dozen activities pulling at him. But it was July, and Tanner and his family were spending a month on the beach in the south of France. The days were long and carefree. In fact, there were no signs that something strange and miraculous was about to happen.

Something that would change Tanner's life forever.

Tanner's sister, Erin, was two years younger than him, but the two had always been buddies. Most days that summer, Tanner and Erin would play Frisbee on the beach and splash in the waves while their parents played tennis at the club or swam at the pool, some two hundred yards away. The Woods family had spent lots of time at the beach—both near their California home and on vacation. But still their parents urged them to be careful.

"Watch for the riptides," Tanner's mother warned them each morning. "You kids are used to the ocean, but keep an eye on each other."

Tanner and Erin loved the freedom of staying at the beach by themselves all day. By midsummer they had each made several new friends along the shore. One afternoon just after lunchtime, a woman and two young blond girls walked down the beach and set up not far from where Tanner and Erin had their towels. Tanner and Erin could tell by the family's fair coloring that they were from one of those Scandinavian countries like Sweden or Norway.

"Must be new," Tanner whispered to his sister. Erin nodded. Neither of them had seen the family before. The teens watched as the two little girls—who looked about seven and four years old—climbed into a rubber raft and set out into the water.

"Wonder if they know about the riptides?" Erin asked.

Tanner narrowed his eyes, his heartbeat twice as fast as before. For the most part, the people playing in the surf had cleared out by then. Tanner studied the waves and immediately understood why. The riptides were back! They came up every day at about this time, but that afternoon they were stronger than Tanner had ever seen them.

He glanced back at the rubber boat and his breath

caught in his throat. The small craft was being sucked out to sea and the young girls were huddled at one end, their faces frantic.

"Look!" He nudged Erin and pointed at the little boat. "Those girls are gonna drown." He jumped up and raced toward the woman who had brought the young girls.

"Tanner!" Erin shouted after him. "Be careful."

But Tanner barely heard his sister's warning. Fear welled up within him and he was breathless when he reached the woman. "Ma'am . . . your girls!" He sucked in a quick breath. "They're in trouble!" He gestured out to the two little girls. Both were screaming, their voices lost on the pounding surf. Their small boat was twice as far out to sea as it had been before.

The woman was on her feet in an instant, panic written across her face. "Girls!" she screamed. "Someone, help!" Hysteria filled her voice and she shot a desperate look at Tanner. "I can't swim!"

Across the beach, Erin was watching the drama unfold. Now she ran across the hot sand and caught up with Tanner just as he bolted for the water. "Tanner!" Her voice was a shriek. "You can't do this. You'll be killed!"

"I have to, Erin. Those girls don't have a chance." Tanner did not hesitate another moment. But as he sprinted for the shore, he turned back one last time. "Pray for me, Erin. Please pray."

"No, Tanner . . . don't go!"

In all her life, Erin had never been so scared. There were no adults around, no time to find her parents. By then a small crowd had gathered near the two girls' mother, comforting her, praying with her. Erin wanted to scream. *What about my brother! What if he dies trying to save those girls!*

At that instant, Tanner ran through the surf and dove into the waves. In a matter of seconds he was caught in the same riptide as the children, his arms cutting powerful strokes into the water as he struggled to reach their rubber boat.

"Tanner!" Erin started to sob. "Don't drown, Tanner. Please!" Panic choked her and she grabbed fistfuls of her hair. Her brother would never make it out alive and all she could do was watch.

Then she remembered Tanner's final words. *Pray for me, Erin. Please pray.* Still terrified, Erin fell to her knees and covered her face with her hands. "Please, God...make a miracle happen for my brother and those girls. Please..."

Meanwhile, some fifty yards offshore, Tanner was breathless at the strength of the current. He fought back the panic that splashed his face with every wave. *Okay, God. I need your help here.* Pausing a few precious seconds, Tanner yanked off his shirt, kicked off his sandals, and kept swimming. Never had the water tugged so desperately at his body. His heart raced and every few seconds he swallowed another mouthful of salt water.

"Girls!" He struggled for a breath of air. "I'm coming!" The water was choppy and only by straining with all his might could he see the rubber boat ahead of him. He fought toward the little craft, one stroke after another. The current was taking him straight for them. He could hear their little-girl screams, and he allowed them to drive him forward. Stroke after stroke. *Don't let me drown, God. Those girls need me.*

When he was ten feet away he silently thanked God. He was going to reach them! That was the good news. The bad news was something that made Tanner's heart race within him. His limbs were beginning to feel numb. He knew the reason why. He was running out of energy.

But somehow he held out. One minute led to two and finally Tanner was at their side. He clutched the edge of the boat and peered inside at the terrified, screaming children. "Girls. It's okay. We're going to be all right."

Tanner wasn't sure if the young Scandinavian girls would speak English, but they did. "Help us! Please!" The older of the two girls scrambled toward him, leaning the rubber boat too far to the side. Both girls screamed and grabbed the sides of the boat as water began pouring in. Tanner worked his way to the other side, desperate for a solution. Every second the riptide was pulling the boat farther out to sea.

"Shh," Tanner told the girls. "Stop crying and stay still. We're going to be all right."

The girls' screams quieted to soft, frightened whimpers.

There was only one way they would make it back to shore. *I've gotta' swim, God. Give me the strength. Give me a miracle.* Tanner took a deep breath and stared at the cluster of people on the shoreline. Somewhere Erin was watching him, praying for him. He summoned the last of his strength, drew another breath, and with one hand still clutching the small boat, he began swimming toward shore.

He was only a hundred yards from the beach, but the riptide was relentless. For three minutes he kicked and pushed against the current, but his efforts only worked to keep the boat in place. The older girl saw his difficulty and began to cry aloud once more.

"We're going to drown!" she screamed.

"No we aren't!" Tanner craned his neck and stared at the child. His tone was calm, despite the panic welling within him. "Sit down next to your sister and be quiet." As the girl grew quiet once more, Tanner was able to focus all his attention on reaching the shore.

Minutes passed and yet it seemed they had barely moved five yards closer to shore. Tanner's legs were cramping, his energy drained. He thought about football and the training drills he'd been through with the team the previous summer. *Tough it out, Tanner. Come on, you can do it!* He could almost hear his coach talking to him over the waves. Or maybe it wasn't his coach.

God? Is that you? Help me! I can't do this!

You can do all things through Christ who gives you strength, Tanner. Don't give up.

This time Tanner was sure it wasn't his coach. He'd heard his favorite Bible verse. It was the same Bible verse that hung on the wall in his room. He'd always said he could do anything with God's help.

Yes, that was it, wasn't it? Tanner kicked furiously, a new strength surging through him. He glanced over his shoulder and saw the two girls, their white-blond hair matted to their faces, their pale blue eyes wide with fright. He would not give up. If they drowned, then he would, too.

Tanner lunged forward with each stroke of his free hand and yanked the raft between strokes. The current was so strong he felt as if he were pulling the raft straight up a hill. Still he continued.

Back on the beach, Erin was still on her knees, still praying constantly for her brother. The crowd around the girls' mother was growing and everyone had left the water except for Tanner and the children. *Come on, God. Get him back to shore. Please!*

Erin studied her brother, her body paralyzed by fear. Tanner was a brilliant swimmer. If it was taking him this long to pull the girls back to shore, something was terribly wrong. Erin had heard of currents that literally pulled people underwater to their deaths. She prayed that this was not the case as she kept her eyes riveted on her older brother.

There were no rescue boats, and although Erin had heard someone call for the local lifeguards, this was a private beach and none had arrived yet. In addition, among the few people who'd gathered, no one looked able to carry off a rescue. No one but Tanner.

"We need you, God. Give us a miracle." Erin's voice mingled with the wind as she once more began to pray.

Out in the water, Tanner knew he had long since run out of energy. His toes and calves cramped with every kick and he was barely able to keep his eyes open. Something besides the current tugged at him, urging him to drop the boat and let the waves have their way with him. But every time he began to sink, the salt water stung his lips and eyes and he fought for the surface once more.

Time blurred as one yard at a time Tanner drew closer to shore. Adrenaline coursed through his body, forcing him forward, even if only a few inches at a time.

Please God, he prayed silently. *Help me get these children back to shore.*

If he gave in to the fatigue that racked his arms and legs, he and the girls would all drown. Even if they didn't, the progress he had made so far would be wiped out in the driving riptide. He pictured his bedroom back home. *I can do all things through Christ who gives me strength.* The verse ran through his mind again and again. He pursed his lips in determination and continued forward.

About that time, Erin heard footsteps behind her. She turned and saw her parents running across the beach.

"Where's Tanner?" her mother shouted from a distance. Her eyes were wide, terrified.

"Is that him out there?" Her father pointed toward Tanner and the girls in the boat.

"Oh, Mom . . . Dad . . . I'm so scared." Erin was in their arms before she had time to explain. "Tanner didn't want them to drown."

"I'm going out, too." Her father took a few steps toward the shore.

"Dad, don't do it!" Erin shouted. "The current's too strong."

"She's right," her mother came up alongside him. "Besides, Tanner's making progress. Don't go in unless he needs you."

For several more agonizing minutes, Erin and her parents waited and prayed, huddled a few yards from the crowd of people around the children's mother. Gradually, Tanner and the girls moved closer to shore. When they were only ten yards away, Tanner's father swam out and pulled the trio safely to the sand.

As the crowd surrounded them and the girls' mother swooped her daughters into a waiting towel, Tanner's father lifted him into his arms and took him onto the beach, where he set him gently in a chair.

"Thank God, you're okay!" Tanner's mother ran alongside them. There were tears of relief in her eyes and in Erin's as they gathered around him. Tanner's hands and legs were swollen and his face was grayish-white. He began to moan.

"Son!" His father wrapped a blanket around him. "Are you all right? Can you hear me?"

Tanner could barely hear his dad's voice. He opened his eyes, but everything was blurred. "Water," he said.

"I'll get it!"

Tanner thought the voice was Erin's, but he was too tired to care. He closed his eyes and slept until he felt his mother gently waking him. She held a bottle of water to his lips. "Here, son. Drink."

After several sips Tanner sat up straighter and opened his eyes fully. He looked around, past his parents and sister toward the area where the little girls' mother had been. The sparse crowd including the girls and their family were already making their way up the beach.

Tanner blinked and shot a look at his parents and sister. "Were the girls okay?"

"They were fine." Tanner's mother ran her hand over his forehead. "They should've at least stopped to thank you."

Tanner shrugged. "Oh, well. They probably

wanted to get the girls indoors. They were pretty scared." He sank back in the beach chair and closed his eyes again. He was exhausted, but he had survived the ordeal and he was humbly thankful. God had pulled him through. Only he knew how close he'd come to giving up and letting his body sink beneath the waves.

Throughout the rest of the week the village people got word of Tanner's heroic rescue and began treating him like a celebrity. People pointed to him and talked in whispers, and several times people came up to him and congratulated him on saving the lives of the young girls.

Tanner learned from several of them that the girls' father was Peter Schilling, a very wealthy merchant in town. Apparently he didn't like Americans and had voiced that to others on more than one occasion. This puzzled Tanner—that the man would put his dislike of Americans over his daughters' rescue—but he tried not to think about it. The man had to have known where Tanner's family was staying, and yet he made no attempt to contact Tanner or to thank him in any way for saving his daughters' lives.

Finally the month drew to an end, and the Woods family packed their things and returned home to Southern California. As they boarded the airplane, Tanner glanced once more toward the airport. He had secretly hoped Mr. Schilling might choose this time to thank him in person for his rescue. But when he saw no one, he decided to put the incident out of his mind.

Fifteen years passed and Tanner finished school and college. His younger sister married and had two children, but Tanner became an attorney and remained single. He dated occasionally, but for one reason or another never wound up in a serious relationship.

"It's time you find yourself a wife, Brother," Erin joked once in a while.

But Tanner would only shake his head. He was more serious than his sister and did not easily make close connections with people. Though girls had always been interested, none of them had captured Tanner's heart.

The summer he turned thirty, he decided to vacation alone at the same spot in the south of France where his family had stayed fifteen years earlier. The anniversary of the day he had rescued the little girls was approaching, and for some reason he felt compelled to spend it on the same beach.

"I don't know what it is," he told Erin. "I feel drawn to that place."

"Something to do with saving those kids?" Erin asked.

Tanner shrugged. "I don't know. It's just something I can't get out of my mind. I have to go back there."

Once there, Tanner stayed at the same hotel and passed the hours thinking about his future. For several days he walked the beach and swam the surf. He made little conversation with anyone and after nearly a week he felt well-rested and ready to return to his life.

Sunday arrived—the fifteen-year anniversary of his miraculous rescue. Late that afternoon Tanner walked down the beach and sat near a tree just up the shore from the spot where the girls had first gotten pulled out to sea. Suddenly he heard someone coming up beside him. He turned and saw a beautiful young woman. Her hair was pale blond and something about her light-blue eyes was hauntingly familiar. He waited until she was beside him before nodding to her. "Hi."

"You're Tanner Woods," she said softly.

Tanner's eyes widened and he stood up, slowly moving toward the woman. "I'm sorry," he said. "Have we met?"

The woman smiled shyly and looked away. "Not formally." She tossed her hair over her shoulder. "My name is Heidi Schilling, daughter of Peter Schilling."

Instantly Tanner understood. "You were in the boat... the day I rescued you!"

Heidi nodded. "I was four years old; my sister was seven. We had just set out for a ride in the waves when the current took us out to sea."

"And before anyone knew what was happening," Tanner continued, "you two were in big trouble."

The young woman was quiet a moment, her blue

eyes glistening from the reflection of the surf. "All my life I've wanted to meet you, to thank you for what you did that day. I know you risked your life to save us."

Tanner couldn't believe it. How incredible that they'd meet after so many years. "So you're nineteen?"

Heidi nodded, a smile playing on her lips.

"How did you know it was me?"

"Townspeople talk. It's a small place and they never stopped telling the story about how Phillip Schilling's daughters were rescued by an American. When you returned, several people remembered you. I was hoping to find you here...since this is the anniversary of that day. When I saw you, and saw that you were American, I took a chance."

Tanner nodded. Her story made sense. He had told some of the people at the resort who he was, and a few of them who had worked there that summer fifteen years ago still remembered the incident. There were only five hundred people in the seaside town, so it was very possible that Heidi would hear about his presence.

Heidi was beautiful, but at that moment, her expression grew sad and distant. "I want to apologize," Heidi said. "For my father. He is a very stern man, stuck in his ways. Sometimes I wonder if he even really cared that you rescued us that day. I know he never thanked you, and all my life I've wanted to do something about that."

Tanner smiled. "Now you have."

Strange feelings were beating at Tanner's heart. Somehow being with this woman made him feel that he'd known her all these years. She was young, no doubt. Just a teenager. But she seemed a decade older. "Could you have dinner?" he asked her.

She grinned, and a hint of red tinged her cheeks. "I'd love to."

The two spent the rest of the afternoon talking about the lives they had lived for the past fifteen years. After dinner they returned to the beach and strolled along the shore, side by side. Tanner learned that Heidi was a very lonely young woman. Her father had never treated her like his other daughter. He had always accused Heidi's mother of getting involved with an American tourist, and he'd decided Heidi was the foreigner's daughter, not his. It was for that reason he hated all Americans.

"That's why he never thanked you." Heidi hung her head for a moment, her hands at her side. "Sometimes I think he wanted me to die that day."

"Heidi, that's awful." Tanner reached for her fingers and took them loosely in his own.

In the years since, Heidi's mother had died, and her sister had married and moved away. Tanner felt his heart going out to the young woman beside him. By the time the evening was finished, Tanner had the strangest sense that he would someday marry Heidi. He made plans to see her the next day and the next. He stayed long beyond the time he'd allotted for his vacation. By the time several months had passed, he shared his feelings with her.

"I know you're young," he told her, taking her hands in his own. "But marry me. Leave this lonely place and come back with me to the States."

Tears filled Heidi's eyes and she made a sound somewhere between a laugh and a sob. "Are you serious?"

"As serious as I was that day when I rescued you."

That evening they shared the news with Heidi's father. He had no comment other than, "Be gone, then." He waved her off with a brush of his hand. "But if you marry the American, don't bother coming back here ever again."

Heidi was sad but not surprised by her father's response. Later that week she and Tanner left for the United States.

Tanner's family could hardly believe what had happened. Tanner had left for vacation a confirmed bachelor and returned two weeks later engaged to a beautiful young woman. But when they learned that she was one of the children Tanner had rescued that summer at the beach, they were stunned. And delighted.

Tanner and Heidi married and in the next few years had a little girl, Amy, who had golden hair and sea-blue eyes like her mother. People who knew the couple often talked about the love they shared, marveling at the way they seemed almost a part of each other.

"Don't you ever fight with each other or have a bad day?" Erin asked Tanner once.

Tanner shook his head. "I was thirty when I met her, but God picked her for me when I was just a teenager," he said. "I guess I'm just making up for lost time. I love her and Amy like no one in my life, Erin. Sometimes I think it's part of what we prayed for that day on the beach."

Erin's voice grew quiet. "I never thought of it that way..."

"I mean, who would've thought? All those years ago I was saving that girl to one day be the love of my life. Back then I knew it was an answer to a prayer that we survived. But now I see it was more than that. It was a miracle, Erin. Nothing short of a miracle."

Save a Place for Me . . .

At age sixteen, Julie Keller wanted nothing more than for her twin brother, Jared, to live another year. One more Christmas, one more spring. One more summer when they could stay up late and play cards, teasing each other about the school year ahead. But that hot August night she found herself in a hospital waiting room begging God for something much more specific.

One more day.

Jared had been born with cystic fibrosis, a debilitating lung disease. It wasn't a question of whether the illness would take Jared's life. It was just a question of when. "If we're lucky, he'll live to his mid-twenties," doctors had told the Keller family.

And Julie's parents agreed. They had lived a life separate from faith and their son's illness only underlined their belief: "God isn't real, prayer doesn't work, and miracles don't happen," their father would say on occasion. "It's that simple."

But Julie and Jared didn't agree. When they were thirteen, they'd been invited to a Young Life camp with some friends from school. There, they gave their lives to God and together they'd found rides to church every week since. As long as Jared was well enough to attend, anyway. And when he couldn't she'd stay by his side. They'd talk about church and about school and all that went on there.

"Keep praying for me, Julie," Jared would say. "I'll be back."

"I won't stop." Julie would hide her tears and smile.

"Save a spot at the lunch table, okay?"

"Okay."

It was a conversation they'd had many times.

In the past month, Jared had seemed to be doing better than ever. He and Julie went to the Young Life camp again, this time as counselors. Their friendship had never been closer than it was those long days, swimming and taking part in a handful of activities day after day.

But the day after they returned home, Jared began coughing. A person with cystic fibrosis lives with the constant threat of pneumonia. By the next day, it was clear that's what Jared had, and their parents rushed him to the hospital. Over the years, Jared had suffered with pneumonia more times than Julie could remember. But this time was the worst any of them could remember. Immediately doctors began antibiotics and placed Jared on oxygen.

That had been two days ago. Now, doctors had just met with the Keller family and told them the situation.

"I can't promise anything," the doctor had told them. "I'm sorry. It doesn't look like he's going to make it this time."

Their parents held on to each other and wept when the doctors left the room. With all her heart, Julie wanted to tell them to pray, to beg God for a miracle. But she'd tried that before and every time her parents shut her down. "We don't believe," they'd tell her. "Don't push your faith on us."

So Julie watched them without saying a word. Finally her mother turned to her, her eyes still wet with tears. "We're going to the cafeteria for some coffee. Wanna come?"

"No . . . I'll wait here." Julie managed a weak smile. "In case Jared needs me." The moment they were gone, Julie exhaled long and slow.

God, she prayed silently, *don't let my brother die. The two of us share everything.* That had been true ever since they were small children, but especially once they entered high school. Julie was a cheerleader, popular and outgoing, with dozens of friends. Jared was quieter, slender and weak from his illness. But because of Julie, he was constantly showered with attention. By the end of the previous year, he'd been named Most Fun To Be With in their sophomore class.

"It's so cool," one of Julie's friends had said the

week before at youth camp, "how you and your brother are best friends. I wish I had something like that with my brother."

Now, after the greatest week together in their lives, it looked like she might lose Jared. The thought tore at Julie's heart and made it hard for her to breathe. She hung her head and let the tears come.

The minutes passed slowly and all Julie wanted was to leave the waiting room and find Jared. Maybe if he heard her voice, felt her hand on top of his... Maybe then he'd find the strength to hang on, even one more day. But the doctor had asked them to stay away for now. He needed his rest if he was going to make progress against the fast-moving pneumonia.

"Lord," Julie whispered. "Please help my brother. I love him so much, and I know he's scared right now. Please help him breathe. Make the pneumonia go away."

At that instant, Julie heard someone enter the room through the open door. She looked up and saw a small man dressed in janitorial clothing pulling a mop and water bucket on wheels. Something about the man's face seemed unnaturally kind, almost glowing. Julie stared at him curiously. His uniform was rumpled, and he was slightly stooped over.

"I have something to tell you," the man said. His voice was so soft, Julie had to slide forward on the vinyl hospital sofa to hear him.

"What did you say?"

"There's something you need to know." The man smiled and again Julie felt warmed by his presence. Did she know him from somewhere? Church, maybe? He took a step closer, his eyes locked on hers. "It's a message from God."

Julie's hands trembled and her mind raced. A message from God? Who was the man and where had he come from? She leaned forward so she could hear him better. Normally she was afraid of strangers, but not this time. The man seemed like someone she'd known all her life. She waited as the man took one more step toward her. His smile was gentle and it calmed her anxious heart.

"Your brother's going to be okay." The man winked at her. "Remember the words from Malachi 4:2."

A dozen questions flashed in Julie's head, but before she could ask one of them, the man turned and left, pulling his mop and water bucket out of the room.

"Wait!" Julie jumped up and raced toward the door. She stepped into the hallway expecting to see the man a few feet away, but he was gone. None of the other doors in the hallway were open. The nurses' station was ten yards down the hallway, but Julie could see only a single nurse standing behind the counter. Julie's heartbeat doubled and her mouth hung open. How had he gotten away so fast? And who was he, anyway? No one could move that quickly, especially pulling a bucket of water.

Julie waited a moment, looking up and down the hallway in both directions, hoping to see him dart out from one of the other rooms. But after a while she turned around and moved slowly back to her seat. How had the man known about Jared? Could he possibly have known that she was waiting for news about whether her brother would live through the night? And what about his message. Malachi 4:2? Julie didn't have her Bible with her, so there was no way to know what the verse said.

After almost a minute, Julie stood up again and headed for the nurses' desk. There was no way she could let the man get away without talking to him, asking him the questions that plagued her. As she walked toward the lone nurse behind the counter, she steadied her voice. This was no time for tears.

"I need to speak with one of your hospital janitors, please." Julie hesitated. "He was small, about this tall." She used her hand to show how high the man had stood. "He stopped by the waiting room here a few minutes ago. I'm not sure where he is right now, but I need to talk to him. Could you page him?"

"Hmmm, that doesn't sound right." The nurse pulled a stapled set of pages from a nearby drawer and scanned it slowly. "That's what I thought." She looked up at Julie, her tone puzzled.

"What?"

"The janitors..." She looked briefly at the paper

once more. "They've all gone home. They left three hours ago."

"No." Julie shook her head. "There must be someone else, another janitor or something. The one I talked to walked right into that room." She pointed toward the waiting room. "I just talked to him three minutes ago. He's somewhere down that hallway."

"Well, all I can tell you, honey, is he doesn't work at this hospital. Our janitors went home. They're all off the clock. Besides, I don't think we have a janitor that fits the description you gave me."

Julie took a step back and turned around. With slow movements, she made her way back down the hall to the waiting room and her place on the vinyl sofa. There she dropped her head in her hands and prayed again. *God, was that for me? That man . . . his message?* She exhaled hard and noticed that her hands were shaking. If he wasn't a janitor for the hospital, who was he? And how had he known about Jared? The questions ricocheted in Julie's soul until she heard someone entering the room again.

She looked up expecting to see her parents, but this time it was Jared's doctor.

"Are your parents around?"

Julie nodded, struggling to find her voice. "They're down in the cafeteria. They'll be right back." She was afraid to ask the next question. "How's Jared?"

A smile worked its way across the doctor's face. "Well, I guess I can tell you." The doctor shrugged.

"It's nothing short of a miracle. Jared wasn't breathing well at all. In fact, ten minutes ago we thought we were losing him. Then he began coughing and in a few minutes he was breathing normally again. We took an X ray, and . . . I can't explain it. His lungs are dramatically better. I've never seen anything like it."

"You mean, he's okay?" Fresh tears filled Julie's eyes.

The doctor's smile faded some. "He's sick, you know that. There's nothing any of us can do about his cystic fibrosis. But he's out of danger. At least for now."

When Julie's parents returned, she shared the good news with them. The joy on their faces was instant and it tugged at Julie's heart. A prayer worked its way silently across her soul. *Thank you, God. You're so good to give us a little more time.*

Then Julie looked from her mother to her father and back again. "Can I tell you something?"

"Of course, dear." Her mother came up alongside her and touched her shoulder.

"I think I saw an angel."

Her mother withdrew her hand and twisted her brow. "An angel? Why, Julie, whatever would make you say that?"

Julie took a deep breath and told them the story about the janitor and his message. For the first time since she and Jared had started believing in God, her parents actually listened. But it wasn't until she got home and checked her Bible that her parents' attitude toward faith changed forever.

The verse talked about revering God's name so that healing would come.

"Even the doctors said Jared's turnaround was a miracle," their mother said later that night. "Who are we to disagree?"

As for Julie, she never forgot how close she came to losing her brother that morning. After that, she always kept the verse about healing tucked away in her heart. She recited it again and again each time she found herself in that lonely hospital waiting room praying for her brother to have one more summer, one more season. One more day. She never had another visit from the mysterious messenger, but she remained convinced that the man had been an angel, sent to reassure her when she needed it most.

Seven years later, when Jared passed away one cool September morning, Julie was at his side, and so were her parents. They were believers now, people who had come to believe in the very real presence of God in their lives. That day Julie spoke the words from that special Bible verse at his funeral service.

"My brother's entire life was a miracle," she told a crowd of several hundred who had come to bid her brother good-bye. "But it took a certain visitor one summer night to remind me that God was in control. My brother's in heaven now and for the first time his healing is complete." Then she looked up toward heaven, tears streaming down her face.

"I love you, Jared. Save me a spot at the lunch table."

Miracle on Two Battlefields

Ben Wiggins had two sisters, but he never knew either of them. The first died at birth. And the second died tragically at age two. He grew up as an only child, and he never forgot how much his parents had lost.

"Don't worry, Mom," he'd tell her when he was old enough to drive. "You'll always have me around. I'm never going anywhere."

Ben's mother, Sarah, would grin sadly and rough up her son's dark brown hair.

"God has taken two of my babies home," she'd say. "But he knows how much a mother can handle, Ben. You're the one he left for me and your father."

But when Ben turned eighteen, he enlisted in the U.S. Army. Not long after, the Gulf War began and Ben was assigned a place on the front line. The idea of losing Ben on a battlefield thousands of miles from home terrified his parents, but they prayed constantly for their son and believed God would protect him.

"Please, God, let us know when he needs our prayers," Sarah would pray each night. "And bring Ben home safely to us. He's all we have left, Lord."

The initial drive of the Gulf War figured to be the most dangerous. A solid line of U.S. troops took their position against Iraq and prepared for battle. Ben was among them, silently praying words of his own. *God, be with me. Let me survive this battle. Please, God.*

Finally, the moment of battle arrived and Ben pressed across the border into Iraq, shoulder to shoulder with hundreds of Army men. The battle that ensued was intense and fast. One hour led to two and it looked as though the U.S. troops would be wildly successful.

During a brief lull in the action, Ben was resting for a second when he felt someone grab his arm. He spun around and looked straight into the eyes of an Iraqi soldier, a teenager like himself. The man had a gun aimed directly at Ben's face.

In angry, short bursts the Iraqi shouted something in a language Ben couldn't understand. Ben stood there, afraid to move. Suddenly the man hit Ben on the side of the face with the butt of the rifle, and pointed in the opposite direction from his squad. Ben had no choice but to start walking.

God! Help me! Please . . .

Several times over the next few minutes Ben considered shouting for help. Instead, he snuck a look behind him every few seconds and realized his squad hadn't noticed his disappearance. That meant one thing: He was on his own, marching at gunpoint toward the enemy's camp.

The Iraqi soldier ordered him up a hill onto a sandy desert bluff where they stopped. Again the soldier barked something at him. Ben blinked, not knowing what to do. His mouth was dry and his heart felt like it had slipped into a pit in his stomach. *God, what's happened? How did I get here? Don't let me die, God.*

At that instant, the soldier kicked Ben and pointed to the ground. Fearing for his life, Ben lowered himself to the dusty ground below. Again the soldier kicked at him, forcing him to lay on his stomach. *This is it, God. I'm not going to make it without a miracle.* A dozen memories flashed through Ben's mind. His high school soccer team celebrating a state title two years earlier, his girlfriend dancing with him at the prom, his parents praying for him before he left.

His parents! That was it! He knew his mother was praying for him every day—she'd promised she would. The Iraqi soldier barked something else and dug the tip of the rifle into the back of his skull. Ben drew a shaky breath, not sure whether it would be his last. Then he closed his eyes, buried his face in the powdery desert dirt, and prayed like he'd never done before. *God, please let my mother know I'm in danger. She should be praying for me.*

* * *

Moments earlier, across the world in Austin, Texas, Sarah Wiggins sat up straight in bed and screamed.

"Al, wake up!" Her voice was frantic and her husband shot up, his eyes wide and disoriented.

"What is it?" he asked breathlessly.

"It's Ben. He's hurt or in trouble. Something's wrong, Al. I can feel it."

Al Wiggins sighed and relaxed somewhat. "Sarah, he's in Kuwait. There's no way you could know whether he was in trouble or not."

Sarah nodded, her heart racing. "Yes, Al. I prayed that God would let me know when he needed our help. Why else would I wake up in the middle of the night?"

Al considered that. He spoke tenderly to calm his wife. "Let's say he is in trouble." He touched Sarah's cheek. "What can we do about it, honey? We're too far away to help him."

"He's on a battlefield, but so are we. All of life's a battle when it comes to good and evil, Al." Sarah's heart rate returned to normal and she sat up even straighter. "There is a way we can help Ben, even now. We can pray for him."

"Okay." Al nodded and took his wife's hands in his. "Let's pray."

Sarah bowed her head and closed her eyes as she began to pray out loud. "Lord, you've woken me from a sound sleep. I just know it's because Ben is in trouble somewhere. I don't know what he needs or where he is, Lord, but you do. Please help him, God. Whatever he needs, whatever danger he's in, please help him. In your holy name, amen."

Back in Kuwait, at that same instant, Ben heard a distinct voice speaking very near his ear.

"Don't worry. You are not going to die today. God is with you."

Ben looked around, but other than the Iraqi soldier, he was completely alone on the desert bluff. The realization sent chills down his arms and he knew that the words were true, even though the tip of the soldier's rifle still dug into his skull. *You're here, God,* he prayed in desperation. *I hear you, I feel your presence. I beg you for a miracle, God . . . please.*

The moment Ben finished praying, the Iraqi soldier shouted another several sentences. Then he yanked the gun away from Ben's head and inexplicably ran down a sandy embankment.

Ben could hardly breathe. He was alive! And for now, at least, the danger had passed. He lay there a minute and tried to calm himself. *Thank you, God. Whatever just happened . . . thank you.* With slow, cautious movements, he stood up and started across the desert to the place where his group of men was still advancing. Ducking low, he ran with every bit of strength he had until he was safely among U.S. soldiers once more.

Not until two weeks later did Sarah learn what had happened to her son. Ben was back at base and because of the strange capture was allowed to call home. As Ben's story began to tumble out, Sarah felt chill bumps along her spine.

"When did it happen, Son?" She held her breath, already knowing what Ben was going to say.

"Two weeks ago."

"No, the time, Ben. I need the exact time."

"The exact time?" Ben thought a moment and then told her roughly the hour that he'd been captured. "That would've been about two in the morning your time."

Sarah's hand flew to her mouth. "I was praying for you, Ben. God woke me up and had me pray for you."

Across the miles in Kuwait, Ben's heart soared at his mother's statement. "I knew it. I prayed for a miracle, Mom. I asked God to let you know I was in trouble. And that's just what he did."

When Life Changed in an Instant

Rain poured from the skies over the town of Santa Fe, New Mexico, that March day, but Michelle Conley's future couldn't have been brighter. She was an intelligent, pretty senior at Southridge High School with dozens of friends and a fiancé whom she loved dearly. Michelle had known Bobby Barrows since the two were kids. Bobby was three years older than her, tall with dark brown hair and serious eyes. They planned to marry sometime after he graduated from college in fourteen months.

"You're so young," Michelle's mother had told her more than once since the couple had gotten engaged. "Sometimes I wonder if you should wait, dear. Go away to school. Take some time."

But Michelle would only give her mother a kind smile. "I've loved Bobby since we were kids, Mom. That kind of love shouldn't have to wait. Besides, we have everything important in common."

Finally, just a month earlier, both her parents and

his agreed that the two of them were ready. They would seek premarital counseling through their church and sometime a year from the upcoming summer they would get married.

There were four days of school left before spring break that rainy Monday afternoon, and Michelle was excited about having a week off. She and Bobby planned to go hiking with some friends one day and take a shopping trip another. It wouldn't be as exciting as some of their other spring breaks had been, but it would be relaxing. And with all the activities of her senior year weighing on her, Michelle was looking forward to some rest.

It was a twenty-minute commute from her house in a mountainous suburb to her job in downtown Santa Fe. As she drove through the rain, her mind raced with all that lay ahead. How quickly the months ahead would pass, how soon she would cross the stage at graduation. Prom . . . the senior trip . . . a summer with Bobby. All of it lay in front of her like a dream come true.

The rain fell harder than before and Michelle flipped her windshield wipers to a higher level. Suddenly she remembered her father's warning as she'd left the house ten minutes ago. "Drive safe, Michelle; the storm's gonna get worse before it gets better."

Because of the weather she took surface streets into Santa Fe. The drive was uneventful until she was about three miles from work. Suddenly her small

Honda began to shake from the force of the wind. Nervous, she looked ahead and saw a stop sign. She slid her foot over to the car's brake. Suddenly everything went black.

Minutes earlier, Jonas Green had stepped out of the auto body shop where he worked to check on the weather. As he gazed toward the sky he was shocked to see a whirling funnel-shaped cloud descending onto the roadway before him.

The Santa Fe area had occasionally experienced a tornado during monsoon season, but it was still too early for monsoons, and the whirling desert windstorms were typically too small to do much damage. Now, Jonas analyzed the funnel cloud before him. It was slender but obviously still strong enough to tear the roof off a building. Jonas looked around and made a quick assessment. Other than the shop, the stretch of roadway in that part of town was surrounded mainly by open fields, so there were no buildings in danger. But the tornado was easily big enough to lift a car in its path.

Jonas tore his eyes from the whirling cloud and scanned the road. It was clear of cars except for a blue Honda, which was slowing to a stop directly beneath the descending funnel cloud. The driver looked to be a young woman, completely unaware of the narrow swirling cloud hovering over her car. Jonas waved at her frantically.

"Tornado!" he shouted.

But at that instant the cloud engulfed the vehicle, picked it up, and flipped it like a child's toy three times in midair. Jeff watched in horror as the force of the wind slammed the Honda into a ditch along the side of the road and then sucked it back into the air once more before slamming it down on its wheels in the middle of an adjacent field. The funnel cloud then turned indifferently and danced across the vacant land toward the open desert, losing strength until it disappeared.

Jonas raced to the phone and placed a 911 call, then ran across the street and into the field toward the battered Honda. Help might be there soon, but Jonas wasn't sure it was necessary. No *one could live through that*, he thought.

Inside the car, Michelle tentatively opened her eyes and saw that she was in the middle of an empty field. What had happened? How had she wound up here? She blinked, wondering if it was some sort of crazy dream. But when she opened her eyes again, she was still there, in the middle of a field.

Suddenly she realized the windows of her blue Honda were gone, and her body lay partway out the empty back frame. Her head rested on the car's twisted trunk, while the rest of her body lay at an awkward angle along the backseat. Her left leg was crushed between the front seat and the door. The metal where Michelle's head rested was sharp and jagged, and Michelle started to pull her head back into the car. But when she tried, a searing pain burned in her back and her body remained motionless. Panic gripped her heart and a wave of terror washed over her. *Move*, she ordered herself. *Get up!* But she lay perfectly still.

"Dear God, help me!"

At that instant a man reached the car. He was breathless and obviously amazed to find the young woman alive. "Don't move, honey," he said. "Everything's going to be okay."

Michelle ignored the man and tried with all her being to lift her head. When nothing happened, she tried to move her feet and her hands. There was no movement at all, only the intense burning in her back.

"God!" she screamed again. "Help me! Please help me!"

"Listen, stay calm." The man stood near Michelle and moved her blond hair out of her eyes. "My name's Jonas and I'll help you until the ambulance gets here. Tell me your name and phone number and I'll call your parents."

Michelle moaned, then choked out the number. The pain was unbearable, and she no longer even noticed the uncomfortable twisted metal beneath her head. "Tell them to hurry . . . please."

Jonas disappeared with the information. Suddenly two more men ran up to the car. One of them leaned toward her and moved a section of hair off her face. "You're gonna be fine, Michelle. Just lay still."

"W-w-what happened?" Michelle's teeth were chattering and she realized the rain was hitting her face.

The other man tore off his jacket and held it over her head. "It was a tornado. Your car was picked up and tossed over here. But you're gonna be okay. Just keep believing that."

"Are you a believer?" the first man asked.

Unable to move her head, Michelle looked at him from the corners of her eyes. There was something strangely peaceful about the man's face. "Yes. I believe. I believe very much."

"Good." It was the second man. "We're praying for you, Michelle. You're going to be okay. Believe that, okay?"

She swallowed, glad that some of the fear was fading. But at that moment, spots began dancing before her eyes and the voices of the men faded away. Before she lost consciousness, Michelle had just one thought. *How did they know my name?*

When she came to, paramedics were working to get her out of the wrecked Honda and she could hear her father's voice.

"Michelle, can you hear me? It's Daddy, honey."

Michelle opened her eyes and saw him standing behind the medical workers. Nearby her mother was crying hysterically. Tears welled in Michelle's eyes. If her mother was that upset, then something must be terribly wrong.

"Dad..." Her voice was barely loud enough to

hear over the sound of sirens. "Please make Mom stop crying."

Her father wheeled around. "You're scaring her, Mary! Please stop crying." After that there was silence.

Michelle tried to move but again there was no response except for a deep burning in her spine. She moved her eyes all about her and saw Jonas, the first man, the one who had promised to call her parents. But the other two men were gone. "Daddy, what happened?" Michelle whispered. "Look at my car."

"Don't worry about your car." He peered between two rescue workers, his eyes damp. "Let's take care of you."

She searched for Jonas again. "Thanks for calling my parents."

Jonas nodded. He looked too sad to speak.

"Where's the other two guys? The ones who came as you were leaving?"

Jonas lowered his brow and shook his head, confused. "I'm the only one who's been here except for the paramedics. No one else is at the shop today."

Michelle closed her eyes once more as the paramedics fitted a brace around her neck. Two other men began using a powerful tool to cut through the window frame and free her from the nearly unrecognizable remains of the Honda. As her limp body was being strapped to a straight board, Michelle overheard paramedics discussing her back injury with her parents.

Suddenly the images that had been in her mind before the accident came back again. *No, God! Not my back. Please don't let my back be broken.* She wanted to beg God to let her walk again, but she was too afraid to form the words. Even in her heart. Things seemed to be happening at a crazy pace around her. A helicopter landed nearby and paramedics rushed her toward it. In the background she could hear her mother crying again, and a burst of panic made it difficult to breathe.

"What about my parents? Can they come?" She was terrified, her throat so tight she could barely speak.

"They'll meet us at the hospital." A paramedic leaned over her. "Try to relax, honey. We'll get you there as fast as we can."

Michelle closed her eyes. As everything began to fade again, she remembered the two men, their calm faces and gentle words. *You'll be okay. Believe that . . . Believe that . . .* How strange it was that Jonas hadn't seen them. And how had they known her name? There seemed to be no explanation, but as she was lifted into the helicopter she felt the peace from their message once more.

When Michelle awoke again, she was in a hospital bed. Out of the corners of her eyes, she could see screws protruding from her temples. Weights dangled from her skull, and she could see that she was strapped to a device that seemed to stretch her body. She could feel none of it.

At that moment, a doctor entered the room and came toward her.

"Hi," she said, her voice groggy. "I'm going to be okay, right?"

"Michelle," the doctor sighed, and moved closer to her. "You need to know the truth. A funnel cloud picked up your car and slammed you onto the ground two separate times. The impact forced you headfirst into the rear windshield, breaking your back and crushing your spinal cord."

Michelle could feel the color draining from her face. "So, how long until I'm better?"

"I'm sorry to have to tell you this, Michelle." He took a steadying breath. "You're paralyzed from the neck down. You will not walk again." Michelle stared at the doctor, her eyes wide. She wanted to scream at him, shout that he was a liar and that she was too going to walk again. Her mind racing, she thought of the two strange men—the ones no one else had seen. Hadn't they said they were praying for her? *You told me everything was going to be okay!*

Before she could think of anything to say, her parents came into the room. Tears streamed down their faces as they watched her take the news. Their defeated expressions told her the doctor had obviously already spoken with them. Michelle swallowed, searching for her voice.

"It's a lie; it's not true," she said, her voice louder and stronger than before. "I will walk again. I'm leaving this hospital and graduating with my class. And I'm going to marry Bobby."

Her mother closed her eyes and buried her head in her husband's shoulder. Her father stroked her hair and smiled at Michelle. "Sweetheart, if anyone can do it, you can."

"Not me, Dad. God." Michelle grimaced at the pain in her neck. "I'm asking God to heal me, and he will. He can do anything."

Her parents nodded. "We're all praying, Michelle," her mother said. "And we'll keep praying until you can walk again. Honey, do you want us to call Bobby in?"

"Please," Michelle whispered. And for the first time since the accident, tears filled her eyes.

Outside in the hallway, Bobby had been at the hospital keeping vigil for Michelle since her arrival the day before. He had listened to the doctors explain her condition, and he still felt trapped in a state of shock. His mind was wracked with despair as he considered their plans for the future and how they had been torn apart in an instant. He and Michelle shared a strong faith in God and attended church together. But it was difficult to see God's plan at a time like this, and he wrestled with his emotions.

He thought about their plans to marry and

Michelle's dream of having a big family. Now she would never walk up the aisle, never bear children, and never share with him the life they had imagined. Instead there was only the harsh reality of Michelle strapped to a wheelchair every day for the rest of her life. He would stand by her, of course. But he knew it would take a miracle to find the strength to do it.

"Bobby." Michelle's mother interrupted his thoughts as she poked her head out of Michelle's hospital room. "She's awake. She wants to see you."

Bobby glanced up and wiped his eyes. Drawing a deep breath, he steadied himself and entered her room.

Michelle's eyes met his, and tears trickled onto her cheeks. "I'm sorry," she sobbed. "Oh, Bobby, I'm so sorry."

Bobby moved next to her and took her lifeless hand in his, placing a finger across his lips. "I love you," he said, his voice soothing and filled with concern. He bent over and kissed her tenderly on the lips, keeping his face inches from hers. "We'll make it through this thing together, Michelle. Everything's going to be all right."

Michelle nodded and looked heavenward. Then she told him about the strange men, the ones no one else had seen. "They told me I was going to be okay. I have to believe it, Bobby. God will heal me. I know he will."

Bobby nodded, and his tears mingled with hers. "We can't ever stop believing."

For three days Michelle tried desperately to move her fingers and toes, with no success. Then, on the fourth day, the doctor decreased the weight on her head, and suddenly Michelle was able to wiggle her right leg and both arms. The doctor's eyes grew wide in amazement, and he summoned another doctor into the room.

"Look at this." He motioned to Michelle to move once more. When she did, the second doctor furrowed his brow and reached for her chart.

"That's impossible." He looked back at Michelle. "X rays show extensive damage to the spinal cord and a break in the vertebrae."

Michelle smiled at the doctors. "God doesn't care about X rays. He's going to heal me. I'll walk again; wait and see."

Later that week Michelle asked her mother to find her Bible, bring it to the hospital, and read it to her. When her mother arrived, her face was less troubled than before. "Listen to this. It's from Psalms 116."

She opened the Bible and began to read:

> I love the Lord because he hears me; he listens to my prayers. He listens to me every time I call to him. The danger of death was all around me; the horrors of the grave closed in on me; I was filled with fear and anxiety. Then I called to the Lord. "I

> beg you, Lord, save me!" The Lord is merciful and good; our God is compassionate. The Lord protects the helpless.
>
> When I was in danger, he saved me. Be confident, my heart, because the Lord has been good to me. The Lord saved me from death; he stopped my tears and kept me from defeat. And so I walk in the presence of the Lord, in the world of the living.

Michelle felt a surge of hope. *So I walk in the presence of the Lord*...How wonderful was that? The Bible verse talked about being rescued by God and walking again! From that point on Michelle clung to the words in that passage and felt certain that she, too, would walk again in the presence of the Lord in the world of the living.

Two months passed, and doctors performed surgery on Michelle's neck, placing her in a halo brace and later other braces to help stabilize her broken back. During that time she continued to amaze doctors by regaining strength and movement during physical therapy sessions.

On May 21, not three months after the accident, Michelle was released from the hospital and given permission to attend her high school graduation in a wheelchair. "I don't need it," Michelle insisted. "I'm going to walk."

The wheelchair never made it out of the car. A week later, using a cane and assisted by her mother, Michelle donned a graduation gown and attended graduation. While her classmates gave her a standing ovation, she hobbled alongside her mother slowly to the high school podium to accept her diploma.

One year later, while tears filled the eyes of family and friends, Michelle walked gracefully down the aisle of their church and married her childhood sweetheart. Her doctors had told her there was no medical explanation for her recovery. "It's a miracle," they said. "We have no other explanation."

"God was merciful and he healed me completely," Michelle told Bobby that night on their honeymoon. "Just like those two strangers said."

Bobby was thoughtful a moment. "Did you ever wonder if maybe they were angels? You know, sent to give you hope that day?"

"I don't wonder, Bobby." A chill passed over Michelle and she smiled. "I *know* they were angels. Everything about my recovery has been a miracle. How else can you explain those guys? They even knew my name!"

Indeed. Two years later, again defying medical understanding, Michelle gave birth to the couple's first child. Today she and Bobby have been married thirteen years and have three children, ages eleven, nine, and three.

Every spring the couple sits the children around the table and tells them the story of Michelle's accident, her visit by the two strangers, and her miraculous recovery. "We should never limit God," Michelle tells them. "Ask him for help even when the situation seems hopeless. I'm living proof that he hears us and he does answer."

A Time to Go Home

From his role as one of the most prestigious men in his community, Brian T. Noble can hardly remember the rebellious teenager he once was. Back then, he had done things his way, regardless of his parents' deep concern for his life and future. He was sixteen when something happened that would change his life forever.

The son of two loving and devoted parents, Brian grew up in New Orleans, Mississippi, where he was blessed with a wonderful childhood. But after reaching his teenage years he grew restless, anxious to experience the wilder side of life. Shortly after his sixteenth birthday, he decided he no longer wanted to stay in school.

"Brian, I absolutely will not hear of you dropping out of school." His mother shook her head, clearly disgusted by the idea.

"But Mom, I wanna be a prizefighter! The guys at school were talking about it and I know I can do it. Give me a chance!"

"A fighter?" She raised a single hand in his direction. Brian knew the sign well. The conversation was over. "No son of mine is going to leave school for prizefighting. Besides, God has a good future for you, Brian. Good plans and a good life. Don't throw it all away."

His father agreed. "Stay in school, Son. Without an education you have no hope for the future. We'll love you no matter what, but think about your life."

Frustration gnawed at Brian over the next few days and his relationship with his parents became more and more strained. Finally, Brian made a plan to run away from home. He waited until school was out for the summer before he set the plan in motion.

"I need to be a man," he told one of his friends before he left. "Gotta see the world for myself...out there on my own."

Brian was an intelligent boy, tall and athletic with a strong sense of survival. Because he had only a few dollars, he knew he would first need to find work. He headed for the outskirts of town, thinking as quickly as he could about what to do next. By the end of the afternoon, he discovered that by watching the railroad cars, he could determine approximately where they were headed.

He watched the station for nearly an hour. As with all train stops, this one was protected by railroad bulls—large, club-bearing guards who kept people from stowing aboard the boxcars. When the trains began moving, the railroad bulls would climb aboard and ride near the front of the train. They were not worried about people stowing aboard while the train was moving, since to do so would have been foolishly dangerous. For that reason, it was rarely attempted.

Brian could imagine the dangers associated with jumping onto a moving train, but he was not afraid. He would wait until the right train was moving and take his chances. If his timing was right, he believed he could run alongside a slow-moving train and jump aboard one of the cargo cars without incident.

Summoning his courage, Brian studied a train that appeared to be heading north out of New Orleans. Perfect. He made his move, knowing that if he missed, he could fall under the train's wheels and be crushed to death. Brian forced himself not to think about the possibilities. At just the right moment, he jumped and landed safely inside the boxcar.

"Easier than it looks," Brian muttered confidently to himself.

Brian used this new mode of transportation several times over the next few days until he got off the train in a small Kansas town. There he saw what appeared to be a traveling carnival set up under a large banner that read "Bluebird's Circus." Hungry and out of money, Brian approached the circus officials and was hired on the spot. He would help set up and tear down the various rides and acts for minimum wage.

Before he left the manager's office, Brian spotted a sign that said, "Fighters needed—go three rounds with a paying customer." The pay was more than Brian could make in a week.

His eyes lit up and he turned back to the manager. "I'd also like to do a little fighting, if you don't mind." He stuck out his chest. "I'm quite good."

The carnival boss looked him over skeptically. "We'll see, son," he said. "We just might be able to use you."

Now that he had found a place to stay and a way to make money, Brian wrote to his parents. His heart ached that night as he thought about his warm home and how badly he missed his mother and father. The next morning he dropped the letter in the mail.

Several states away, Brian's parents were together when they received an envelope addressed in their son's handwriting. For days, they'd been worried sick. Police had been contacted, but Brian was too old for a state-funded search. "He's a runaway, ma'am. Lots of kids run away. Your best bet is to hope he comes back."

Of course, Brian's parents did more than hope. They prayed constantly, begging God to give them a sign that their son was all right. That day as they stared at the envelope, Brian's father's hands began to shake. This was the answer they'd been looking for.

They opened the letter together, tears gathering for both of them. "You read it." Brian's father handed the letter to his wife.

She took the piece of paper, unfolded it, and in a

shaky voice began to read. "Dear Mom and Dad... I'm sorry for leaving without saying good-bye, but I knew you wouldn't let me go. I can't tell you where I am, but I'm safe...and I might even get to do some prizefighting."

Over the next eight months, Brian traveled with the Bluebeard Circus to dozens of towns from Missouri to Nebraska. Eventually the circus leader allowed him to participate in the pit fights, in which two men were placed in a sunken pit and allowed to fight until one dropped from the punishing blows or from exhaustion. Brian didn't lose a single fight. Each time he won, he would go back to his sleeping quarters, pull out some paper, and write a letter to his parents.

"I think you'd be proud of me," he would write. "No, I'm not in school. But I'm living out my dream. Please don't worry about me."

Meanwhile, Brian's parents could do nothing *but* worry about their son. They had always provided such a steady environment for him, and now he was a drifter, a roustabout and a fighter. They prayed for Brian daily, begging God to keep him safe and bring him home soon.

In February, after a cold Nebraska winter took its toll on carnival attendance, the Bluebeard Circus folded. Brian had enough money to take care of himself for a while. But he wanted to return south and didn't want to cut into his savings by paying for train fare. Resorting to his former method of travel, he stowed away on a series of trains until two weeks later he was in Hayti, Missouri.

After a large lunch at a local diner, he considered his options. Returning home would be admitting failure. He wanted to find another circus, somewhere he could resume fighting. That afternoon Brian talked with local residents and learned that the nearest traveling circus was about twenty miles south. He knew just the train to take him there, and he hid under the loading dock near the railroad station's warehouse, waiting for the perfect moment.

As he crouched in the shadows, he noticed that two locomotives were being hooked up to the train. That meant the train would pick up a great deal of speed much more quickly than usual. It might even be traveling close to full speed as it left the station. *That's okay*, he told himself. He'd jumped on fast-moving trains before. He could do it again. There was nothing to be afraid of.

When the train started to move, Brian ran toward the boxcar and jogged alongside it. Suddenly, the ground beneath him narrowed and he found himself sprinting alongside a steep ravine. He looked ahead and saw that the land was about to drop off at a point where the tracks became a bridge. Panic welled up within him. Why hadn't he noticed the bridge before? There was no time to think about the situation. He had just one chance. If he missed, he would fall into the canyon to certain death.

Without waiting another moment, Brian jumped. At first he grabbed hold of the floor of the boxcar, but at the same time the train picked up speed and Brian lost his grip. He slipped, sliding out of the boxcar and gripping the edge with his fingertips. His body dangled dangerously over the edge and inch by inch he felt his fingers slip.

"No!" he shouted. "Please, God! Don't let me die here!" But Brian knew there was no way to survive the situation. He was seconds from plunging over the edge of the canyon—seconds from death. The muscles in his arms were burning.

Everything his parents had told him in the months before he ran away came rushing back. *We'll love you no matter what, Son . . . Stay in school . . . God has a plan for your life . . .*

At that instant he opened his eyes. Though the boxcar had appeared empty only seconds earlier, in front of him now stood a tall, well-muscled black man, about the same age as Brian's father. The man stared at him intently. "It's time to go home, Brian."

Before Brian could utter a word, the mysterious man reached down, grabbed Brian's hands, and pulled him into the speeding boxcar. Brian's sides heaved as he lay facedown on the floor of the car trying to catch his breath.

He closed his eyes and uttered a silent prayer, still stunned that he was alive. *God, you rescued me.*

How can I thank you? How come I didn't notice that man before?

Brian swallowed hard and found the strength to lift his head. He needed to thank the man. But as he looked around, he heard himself gasp. The man had vanished. The boxcar was completely empty. One of the two side doors was closed, as it had been since the train began moving. He glanced outside and shuddered. There was no way the man could have jumped from the train and survived. He had simply disappeared from sight. Brian sat down slowly in a corner of the car and began to shiver.

Suddenly he knew with great certainty that whoever the man had been, his message had been right on. Brian needed to get home. He stayed on the train until it reached New Orleans and immediately returned to his parents' home.

After a tearful and happy reunion, he told his parents about the man on the boxcar.

"An angel, Son," his father said as his mother took them both in her arms.

"God was watching out for you," she said. "See, he brought you home to us."

Brian nodded. "Things are going to be different now. You watch."

Brian returned to school that week and a few months later, his faith renewed, he was baptized in the local river. After graduating, he moved to Southern California where he spent two years working as a professional prizefighter before being drafted. Brian served in World War II with the Navy. He took part in twenty-eight combat missions in the South Pacific, and after the war he returned to New Orleans, where he became a minister with one of the largest congregations in the city.

Never again did he see the black man who rescued him that terrifying afternoon. But Brian is convinced that his father was right. Not only did God have great plans for his life, but he assigned Brian a guardian angel to make sure those plans would be carried out.

"My entire life would be different if it weren't for that single afternoon," says Brian, whose faith and love for God is always evident these days. "I was a teenage boy with no direction, and God used that angel not only to save my life but to change it into something that could glorify him forever."

On God's Strength Alone

Krista Barrows loved to shop. Even more, she loved that these days she could drive to the mall by herself. No more waiting on friends for rides, no more begging her parents if they'd take her shopping. Just after her seventeenth birthday, she'd bought a used Toyota, and now, with her parents' permission, she was free to shop whenever the need arose.

In fact, life was just about perfect that Christmas season. She attended North Bay High School in San Francisco, where she played flute in the marching band and had recently had the lead role in the school's fall drama production. North Bay was small and Krista knew just about everyone. She was a junior and could hardly wait for her senior year.

It was a week before Christmas and Krista needed to do some shopping. She wanted to buy presents for her parents and two brothers, and something small for her teachers. Then there were half a dozen close friends who planned to exchange gifts with her.

But the present she was most excited to find was an engraved picture frame for her boyfriend. The two knew each other from their church's youth group and they'd been friends for years. They'd only started dating in the past few months, but Krista wanted to find him something special for Christmas.

As she drove to the mall late that afternoon, Krista ran through the things she needed to find. As much as she loved shopping, she hoped she could finish buying for her list before the stores closed.

The hours passed quickly, though, and Krista still had three more presents to find when the mall announced it was closing. She picked up her pace. How had it gotten so late? She hated being at the mall when it closed, not just because it made her feel rushed but because it wasn't safe. Her parents had warned her just that afternoon.

"If you'll be out late, take a friend." Her mother had patted her hand, her smile warm and gentle. "Mall parking lots are dangerous after hours, especially during the holidays."

The warning rang through Krista's heart as she headed for the cash register. In ten minutes she'd made it through the line, gathered three bags in her arms, and dug through her purse for her car keys. *Hurry, Krista,* she told herself. Why hadn't she brought her mother's cell phone? That way she could at least call and tell them she was on her way. They were probably worried sick about how late she was out.

Outside, Krista walked across the dark, cold parking lot, still fumbling for her keys. Lost in her search, she barely noticed in her peripheral vision something move up ahead near her car. Finally her fingers wrapped around her keys and she looked up. The parking lot was nearly empty. Why had she parked so far away? She glanced about, her heart beating faster than before. Then she picked up her pace.

In daylight, she might not have worried about her safety in such a situation. But now, in the pitch dark and all alone in the parking lot, Krista was suddenly frightened. Trying to stay focused, she took quick steps toward her Toyota, opened the door, and climbed inside.

Suddenly, a masked man appeared a few feet from her window. His eyes were wild and he was pointing a gun at her. He took a few hurried steps toward her car, and motioned for her to open the door. With trembling hands, Krista locked her door and tried to start her car. Nothing happened. The man banged his gun against her window as Krista turned the key again. Again, silence. The engine was completely dead.

"Please, God!" she whispered. "I need your help!"

The man smashed the gun against her window another time, this time cracking the glass. Closing her eyes, Krista tried once more to start the car, and finally the engine turned over. In an instant, Krista slammed the car into gear and sped off, leaving the man in the shadows.

Krista cried the entire way home. What had the man wanted from her? And how long had he been waiting by her car? Even stranger, why hadn't her car started the first time she turned the key? The engine was in perfect condition, according to their family's mechanic. *Whatever happened back there, God, thanks for getting me through it.*

She was still shaking when she pulled into her driveway, shut off the engine, and headed up the walkway. A shudder worked its way through her as she imagined the things that man might have done if he'd been able to break her window and get inside. Still feeling weak, she made her way inside. There she tearfully shared the incident with her parents.

Immediately, her father called the police. When he'd made a report, he turned to Krista. "You're safe now," he told her as he hugged her tight.

"But I thought..." Krista's crying became sobs.

"God was looking out for you, honey." Her mother reached out and took her hand. "He helped you get away...I have no doubt about that."

Krista's father cocked his head. "You say the car wouldn't start?"

"Right. It was weird, Dad. It was like it was broken or something."

"Let's go take a look at it." Her father grabbed a flashlight and led the way back outside to where Krista's Toyota was parked in the driveway. "I can't understand why it would have done that. The mechanic just checked it out a few weeks ago."

"I know. I thought it was strange, too." Krista stood beside him, her knees still shaking from the close call with the masked man.

Her father opened the hood and aimed the flashlight inside. For a long while he stood there, saying nothing. Then he took a step back as the flashlight fell slowly to his side. His eyes were wide, his mouth open.

"What's wrong?" Krista looked from her father to the car and back again.

"It's impossible," he muttered.

"What?" Krista moved closer, looking under the car's hood.

"There." Her father pointed the flashlight once more at the engine. "The battery is gone."

"What?" Krista was confused. "Can a car run without a battery?"

A strange chuckle came from her father. "That's just it. It's impossible."

"So how did I . . . " Krista's voice trailed off.

Her father shook his head and lifted his eyes to hers. "Don't you see? Someone set you up. While you were shopping, someone took your battery and then waited for you. They knew you wouldn't be able to start your car and . . ." Her father stopped mid-sentence and Krista guessed he was imagining what the masked man had intended.

"It's impossible," he said again.

"I don't understand," Krista said. She was more confused than ever, and terrified at her father's discovery. She had been set up and yet somehow she had escaped being attacked. "If the battery is gone, how did the car start, Dad?"

"That's what I mean. There isn't any way to start this engine without a battery."

Chills made their way down Krista's spine and she reached for her father's hand. "What are you saying?" she asked softly.

"I don't know. I can't explain it. Somehow you made it home without a battery. It's impossible."

Suddenly Krista felt a peace wash over her. "Could it be God was watching out for me?"

Her father's eyes widened and a knowing look came over his face. Slowly, deliberately, he stared up at the star-covered sky. Krista followed his example, and for several minutes they gazed into the night. Finally, her father broke the silence. "God, we may never understand what happened tonight," he whispered. "But we are eternally grateful. Thank you."

A Heavenly Reminder

When her mother presented her with the idea, Ashley Payton was anything but excited.

"Wyoming!" she whined, her hands in the air. She was a nineteen-year-old minister's daughter who had grown up in Southern California. Beaches, sunshine, and city life was something she took for granted and enjoyed. "I hate country life, Mom. There's no way I'm going to Wyoming."

The plan, her mother explained, was for Ashley to meet up with one of their church friends in Wyoming, where she would join an eight-member Christian singing group called Alive. If the week in Wyoming went well, she could travel with the group across the country, visiting churches for one year.

"It'll be good for you, Ashley." Her mother sounded confident. "At least think about it. You've been looking for a way to get out of town, haven't you?"

"Out of San Bernardino, yes. But I was thinking something more like New York or Chicago." She huffed hard. "Not Wyoming."

But secretly, Ashley's mother had her thinking. Hadn't she always wanted to sing on tour? Was this trip—even if it started off in Wyoming—God's way of letting her have her dream? Ashley pictured herself standing in the spotlight, singing for thousands of people every night. She was blonde with brown eyes and her voice easily rivaled any of the professional recording artists. Maybe this was the break she was looking for.

But what if they didn't play to large crowds? What if the tour stayed in small towns for an entire year? Ashley shuddered at the thought. She had lived in Southern California since junior high and knew how much she would miss her friends. It was a big risk. But Ashley also loved to sing. She had dazzled local audiences since she was four years old and had occasionally been approached by talent agents.

She'd even developed a fanlike following among the large congregation where her father was minister. And though she was not quite ready to cut an album, the idea of singing nearly every night for a year was enticing. Finally, the possibility of getting her dream off the ground loomed larger than her concerns about the small towns.

"Okay," she told her mother a few days later. "I'll do it."

Her mother's face lit up. "Really?"

"Yes." Ashley swung her hair over her shoulder. "Maybe this is the break I've been waiting for."

"The break you've been looking for?" Her mother wrinkled her nose. "This trip isn't about getting discovered, Ashley. It's about serving God with your gift of music."

Ashley gave a short laugh. "That's what I mean."

"I hope so." Her mother hesitated for a moment and leveled a serious look at her. "Without the right mind-set, you'll be nothing but disappointed by a trip like this."

Ashley knew her mother was right, but privately she was certain this trip would break her music career open. Yes, she would be using the gift God gave her. But couldn't she get discovered at the same time? Ashley was certain she could.

A month later, Ashley flew to Wyoming and met up with the rest of the Alive singing group. Fred and Rita were the couple in charge, and they treated Ashley like a daughter. Despite the lack of city luxuries, Ashley sang as lead vocalist at a different church every night that week. She was hooked. And besides, once the group set out on its national tour they would spend time in bigger cities. Certainly the audiences would be bigger, too.

At the end of the trial period, Ashley flew home, spent a week packing, and after bidding her family and friends farewell she flew to meet the group in

Baton Rouge, Louisiana. The group traveled from one city to the next in Fred and Rita's motor home. Each night they would sing at a different church, hoping to soften the hearts of those in attendance. Typically, when the performance was over, they would collect small donations that would pay their food and gasoline costs until they reached their next destination.

For the first few weeks, Ashley could hardly contain her excitement. Not only was she singing with a professional group, touring the country, but night after night she was watching people come to know God. The experience gave her an indescribable joy. God had a purpose for her life, and she could hardly wait for each night's concert.

But as time passed, the joy of singing began to wear thin. Not only that, but the group's meager accommodations began to irritate Ashley. More often than not she found herself thinking about the inconvenience of sharing a motor home with seven other people rather than the joy of singing.

There were occasional tire blowouts and breakdowns and times when the group's funds ran so low there was no telling where their next meal would come from. In addition, Fred was being far too generous with their cash. If a needy person crossed their path, he would use a portion of the group's dinner money to buy the guy a sandwich.

"God knows what we need." Fred would smile at the others. "He'll take care of us."

Even though they had never gone without, Ashley was still bothered by Fred's generosity. One afternoon, three months into the tour, the group stopped at a small southern seaside town for an Italian dinner. Weeks had passed since they'd eaten anything other than fast food, but the previous night's offering had brought in enough that Fred decided they could afford a sit-down dinner.

As the group approached the restaurant, they noticed a man dressed in tattered rags. His weathered face and matted hair were covered with a layer of silt and dirt. He was sitting just outside the restaurant door, his hat in his hands.

"Bum!" Ashley whispered to herself. People like that were so disgusting. Then she had another thought. *Watch Fred invite him to dinner.*

As the group drew closer to the man, Fred stopped and started a conversation with the man. Ashley was horrified. She drew closer so she could hear what they were saying, and she was suddenly assaulted by a pungent smell. It was a mix of the man's body odor and the smell of musty alcohol on his breath. Stepping away, Ashley studied the man from a distance. It must have been months since his last shower. *Disgusting,* she thought to herself. *The man has no pride in himself whatsoever!*

In the course of three minutes, while the rest of the group stood in a cluster behind him, Fred managed to get the man's story. He'd been living on the streets for the past year and needed money for food.

Fred smiled and Ashley knew what was coming. Fred didn't believe in giving people money for food. He believed in giving them food.

"I can't give you any money," he said, a smile playing across his face. "But you could be our guest at dinner tonight. Our treat."

The homeless man looked skeptical. "You wanna bring me the food out here?" he asked. It was obvious he couldn't believe that Fred might actually want a person like himself to eat with his group.

"No, of course not!" Fred waved toward the restaurant door, where the manager was watching them. "Come in! Eat with us."

Ashley wanted to cover her face with a bag. What was Fred thinking? Letting them be seen at a sit-down restaurant with a shabby old homeless man? The grizzly old guy stared at the members of the group and his eyes fell on Ashley. "Okay." He looked back at Fred. "Thanks."

"What's your name?" Fred asked as they moved inside.

"Gus."

Ashley dropped to the back of the group and rolled her eyes in frustration. Now they'd have to smell this filthy man for the next hour and no one would enjoy the meal. She shook her head and followed the others into the restaurant. Maybe she should call home and find a way to pull out of the group. Nothing about the tour was working out like she'd hoped.

Once inside, the manager showed them to a table near the back of a large private room. Ashley sat down first and waited for others to fill in around her. When everyone had found a seat she was horrified to see that the place beside her was still empty. The homeless man still stood off to the side, unsure of whether he should really join the group at a formal dinner table. He looked embarrassed as he scanned his ragged and torn clothing.

"I'll just go outside and wait," he said suddenly. "You can bring me something out there if you want."

Fred stood up and shook his head. "Absolutely not." He pointed to the seat beside Ashley. "Sit there . . . we have plenty of room."

Ashley's eyes grew wide. *Great. Sit him by me.* She slid her chair a few inches from the place where Gus was sitting down. Anger and frustration swirled across her heart and she bit her lip. *Some life-changing music tour this turned out to be, huh, God? I should've just stayed home.*

As the homeless man beside her settled into his chair, a putrid aroma moved like a cloud over the place where Ashley sat. The man smelled so bad, it'd be a miracle if she didn't lose her appetite. Gritting her teeth, she determined to ignore him and enjoy her meal. After all, it could be weeks before they might afford a nice dinner out.

When the waitress had taken their order, Gus looked at Fred and cleared his throat. "Where are you people from?" He barely made eye contact before letting his gaze fall to his lap.

In spite of everything, Ashley found herself feeling almost sorry for him. The guy looked like he didn't have an ounce of self-esteem. She stared at him from the corner of her eye. Where did he spend his nights anyway? In an alley somewhere? How awful would that be?

Ashley blinked back a wave of remorse. Oh, well. It was probably his own fault. Too much drinking or drugs. *He must've done something wrong. People don't just wind up on the streets.*

Fred smiled. "We're a traveling Christian singing group. We call ourselves Alive."

The homeless man's eyes lit up. "A professional singing group? Really?"

"Yes." Fred grinned at his wife. "We're professional."

Ashley pretended to study her silverware. Professional? How could he call them a professional singing group when they could barely afford to eat? And what about their sleeping arrangements? The motor home they were staying in was a far cry from the luxurious hotel suites Ashley had pictured before the trip.

"So you say you're Christians, huh?" Gus asked. He lowered his eyebrows doubtfully. "Well, Christians, I have a few questions for you." The man waited until everyone, even Ashley, was watching him. "You people talk about how much God loves me. How am I supposed to believe that? Look at me, living on the streets. If God loves me why doesn't he get me off the streets?"

Fred looked around at the group. When no one spoke up, he turned toward Gus.

"Well, Gus, God's love doesn't really show up in fine clothes and comfortable lifestyles." He folded his arms, his words slow and easy. "But I can prove God loves you."

"Okay." The man grunted. "Prove it."

"Have you heard about Jesus?"

The man nodded.

"Jesus died for you, Gus, did you know that?" Fred cocked his head, his eyes shining with sincerity.

Ashley studied Fred, amazed at the man's faith

"Jesus, huh?" Gus let loose a shaky sigh. "I've heard about that, but I guess it never really made much difference to me."

At that moment, Rita began to speak. "If you were the only person in the whole world, Jesus still would have died for you. He loves you that much." She reached out and took Fred's hand, her voice soft. "Of course it's up to you, whether you want to believe or not."

Two of the other group members nodded in unison. "You know why He died on the cross, right?" one of them asked.

Gus shook his head. "Not really."

As the conversation continued, Ashley forgot Gus's dirty condition and became deeply interested.

She had never known anyone who understood so little about God. She was a pastor's daughter, after all. She took for granted that everyone had been exposed to the same type of upbringing she'd been given. She turned in her chair so she could get a better look at Gus.

"Jesus died to pay the price for our sins," Fred said simply. "Basically, because of Him you're a free man, Gus."

"A free man? I've always been free."

"Not really," Ashley cut in. The others looked at her in surprise as she turned to Gus again. "When we're free in Christ, our circumstances don't really matter anymore. All that matters is that he's with us, he loves us, and he'll see us safely home in the end."

The moment Ashley finished speaking she realized what she'd just said. *Our circumstances don't really matter anymore?* Was that the way she'd been feeling on this singing tour? The conversation around her grew dim as she stared at her lap. She'd been silently complaining for weeks now, grumbling about the cramped quarters in the motor home and the other inconveniences of living on the road.

The truth was she'd forgotten her mother's words about going on the tour for all the right reasons—as a way of using her gift of song to touch hearts for God. Instead it had been all about her. How comfortable she was...how many people wanted to see her sing... how much money they raised in the process. Now this man sat beside her, hungry for a kind of truth she had taken for granted since she was a kid. Tears stung her eyes and she closed them, ashamed at herself. *Forgive me, God. What have I done? Judging people like this... this poor homeless man. Thinking I'm better than everyone else. I'm so sorry, God. Really.*

For the next thirty minutes the group members took turns sharing their personal stories with Gus, the reasons why they had come to believe, and the certainty that God still heard their prayers and worked miracles among them.

"Miracles, huh?" There was a sudden twinkle in Gus's eyes. "I believe in miracles, too."

By the time dinner arrived, the weary old man seemed to understand. For the first time since they'd met him that evening, hope played across his weathered face. Hope where only an hour before there had been none.

"Come with us," Fred said as the group prepared to leave. "We'll take you to the next town. There's a big church there and we'll set you up with someone who can help you."

"You'd do that? For me?" The corners of Gus's mouth worked their way into a smile.

"Definitely." Fred patted Gus on the back. "Come with us."

Gus nodded but this time he glanced at a clock on the wall. "I need to use the facilities first." He stood and took slow steps toward a restroom nestled in the back of the room. The group waited a few minutes, and then some more. Finally Fred stood up. "I'm going to make sure he's all right. He might need help."

The others got up at the same time and agreed to meet Fred and Gus out in front of the restaurant. Outside, they chatted about the dinner and the way God's truth had touched Gus's heart. After several minutes, they began checking their watches and staring back inside the restaurant.

"What's taking so long?" Ashley peered through the glass looking for a sign of Fred and Gus.

Rita was about to go back in after the two men when suddenly Fred darted out the front door, his face a mask of confusion.

"Did he come out this way?" Fred found Rita, his eyes searching hers. "I can't find him anywhere."

Rita shook her head. "We haven't seen him. Did you check the other exits?"

"The manager said there's an emergency exit in the back near the cook's station. But not in the room where we were eating. The only way out was the way we came in."

"Did you look in the restroom?" Rita crossed her arms, and Ashley and the others formed a half circle behind her.

"I started there. We all watched him go in, and there's no way he could've gotten out without us seeing him. There's only one window in the bathroom and it's near the ceiling. Much too small for a man to climb through."

"You're sure he's not in there?" Rita tilted her head, clearly confused.

"I checked each stall. Then I went to the kitchen." Fred shook his head. "They said they would've noticed a stranger walking through there. They hadn't seen anyone matching Gus's description all night. And not a single customer had been in the kitchen."

"So you thought maybe he came out this way?"

"It doesn't make sense." Fred anchored his hands on his hips. "All of us saw him go into the restroom. He couldn't have come out without getting past us and none of us saw him leave. But I had to ask. Just in case."

The group members scanned the length of the street and shook their heads.

"I'm sure he hasn't been out this way." Ashley stepped forward. "Where could he be, Fred? It doesn't make sense."

Fred walked back into the restaurant and went up to the manager, whose desk was just inside the doorway.

"Have you seen a man with sort of old, ripped clothes and—"

"You mean the bum you brought in here?" The manager frowned. "I've been here for the past half hour. He hasn't come out this way since he went in to eat."

Fred returned to the group outside and sat on a nearby brick wall. There were only two ways out of the restaurant—through the front door or through an emergency door in the back of the kitchen. No one had seen Gus near any of those exits.

"I can't understand it. It's like he just disappeared." Fred scanned the sidewalk, still looking for a sign of the old man.

Suddenly, a heart-stopping possibility washed over Ashley. "You don't think, maybe . . ." She grew silent. Her father had talked about angels once in a while in his sermons.

"They're real," he'd told his children once a long time ago. "Because God says they're real."

Fred looked at her for a moment and then understood. "You mean, maybe he was an angel?"

Ashley nodded, and a wave of goose bumps rose across her arms and legs. "It's possible, isn't it? I mean the guy asks us about God and helps us—" She glanced at the others. "Well, helps me, anyway, remember why we're doing this singing tour in the first place. Then, poof! Just like that he disappears. Sounds like an angel to me."

Fred gazed at Ashley. "I guess we'll never know."

But Ashley was convinced. God must have sent the man to remind her of her purpose—not just her purpose while traveling with Alive, but her purpose in life. After their encounter with Gus, Ashley was able to finish the tour without once grumbling about her comfort. In fact, the trip wound up being life-changing, just like Ashley had hoped.

But not in the way she had expected.

Angel in a Police Car

The prom was everything Kara Spelling had dreamed it would be. She and her boyfriend danced and laughed and talked until late in the night. Now it was after one in the morning and time to drive back down Interstate 17 to their homes in Camp Verde, Arizona. Kara was just a junior that year and her boyfriend didn't have a car. But the prom was an hour north in Flagstaff and her parents had agreed to let her drive if she was careful.

"Be careful." Her father had kissed her on the forehead before she left. "You look beautiful, honey. I know it'll be a night you'll never forget. But make sure you watch yourself on the way home."

Kara's parents were less nervous about the drive than they might've been because it involved all freeway miles. Another common two-lane route ten miles west of the freeway had been the site of dozens of head-on collisions. Many of them fatal.

"The freeway is much safer, dear." Her mother

had smiled as they pulled away the day before. "Make sure you take the freeway and you should be just fine."

Although several of Kara's classmates had chosen to drink at the prom and stay in rented hotel rooms at the place where the prom was held, Kara hadn't drunk anything but water. As she climbed into the car, she kicked off her high heels and tossed them in the backseat. Then she smiled at her boyfriend, Thane. "I'm glad we don't drink." She grinned at him. "It's so stupid. Those guys'll throw up all night and not remember a bit of what happened at the prom."

"I know." Thane slid into the car beside her and buckled the belt. "It's a good feeling…having fun and remembering it. Besides," he laced his fingers between hers. "I feel good doing the right thing."

Kara nodded and pulled out onto the main road. "You tired?"

Thane yawned. "Yeah, I guess."

"Go ahead and sleep. I'm fine." Kara cast him a quick glance. "Besides, it's an hour back home. You might as well get some rest."

Five minutes later she entered Interstate 17 north and settled back in her seat. Thane wasn't a Christian, but he was heading that way fast. A long time ago he had partied with the wilder crowd. But then he met Kara and her friends and started going to church with them. Before long, Kara and Thane were dating. Nothing serious, but enough to be considered an "item."

Every day Kara prayed for Thane—that God would get his attention and help him make a decision to believe. He was close to that; he had to be. Otherwise, why did he help her serve meals at the homeless shelter in nearby Cottonwood each Tuesday night? *Whatever it takes, Lord,* she would pray. *Just make him believe in you. Whatever it takes.*

Kara thought about that prayer now as she took a quick look at Shane. They'd only been driving ten minutes and already he was sound asleep. He was so cute, she thought. So tall compared to the other junior guys.

She stared at the freeway ahead of her. She'd been driving for almost a year and already this stretch of interstate felt as familiar to her as the streets around her home. Her sister was in her first year at Northern Arizona University in Flagstaff, so Kara and her parents had made the trip often. Especially that past year.

Kara drew in a slow breath and felt herself relax. The interstate was wide and safe, but utterly remote. There were stretches where she would drive fifteen miles without even an exit to break up the monotony. A monotony that was worse at night when the Arizona desert spread out on either side of her, vast and pitch dark.

A yawn came out of Kara and then another. Kara shook her head and slapped her cheeks lightly. She was more tired than she'd thought. She turned on the radio and opened her window a crack. *There . . . that oughta do the trick.*

And it did for another ten minutes. But less than halfway home, she closed her eyes for just a moment and her head began to drop. Suddenly she jerked it back up again, her eyes wide open, her heart racing. What had she almost done? She shot a look at her speedometer. She was going seventy-five miles per hour. If she'd fallen asleep . . . She couldn't finish the thought. If she were that tired, she'd have to pull off onto the side of the road and get some ice water, anything to keep her awake. But how many miles would it be until then? Ten? Twenty?

"Come on, Lord." She whispered the words, her heart pounding so hard it was difficult for her to speak. "Keep me awake. Just until the next rest stop."

Less than a minute later, Kara felt herself nod off again. At about the same time, she saw flashing lights in her rearview mirror. She swallowed hard as she realized the lights belonged to a police car. *Great. I must've been swerving.* Again, her heart raced. Thank you, God . . . even if I'm in trouble. At least I didn't kill us.

As Kara pulled over, she wondered where the officer had come from. There had been no traffic on the interstate for miles, and the area she was traveling was practically deserted. Kara looked down and remembered that she was driving barefoot. She thought about reaching into the backseat and grabbing her shoes, but it was too late. She poked at Thane as she parked the car on the side of the road.

"What . . . where are we?" He opened his eyes and squinted as he saw the flashing lights behind them.

"I got pulled over." She rolled down the window and waited for the officer to approach.

As nervous as Kara was, her relief was greater. She was wide awake now, but what would've happened if the officer hadn't pulled her over? A uniformed man walked toward her car and shone a flashlight just high enough so he could see her face. Kara had never been pulled over before. She hoped her parents would understand.

"Good evening, Officer," Kara said as the patrolman stopped beside her open window.

"Are you alright?" The officer bent over and looked at Kara. Something about his face seemed peaceful, almost unearthly. She noticed that his badge number read 37—the same number she wore for her high school's basketball team.

"Yes, sir. I'm fine."

The officer laughed. "Go ahead and put your shoes on. You'll be safer that way."

Kara felt her heart skip a beat. Her shoes? How had the officer known about her shoes? Beside her, Thane reached into the backseat, grabbed her pumps, and handed them to her. She shot him a silent thank-you and slipped them on. But before she could ask the officer how he'd known she was barefoot, he spoke again.

"You've been driving a long way and it's late. You almost fell asleep out there, didn't you?"

"Why . . . yes." Again Kara was stunned. It was like he could read her mind, like he'd been riding beside her the entire time. "Our prom went later than I thought and, well, I guess I'm pretty tired." She met his eyes again and noticed that he never blinked. She exhaled slowly. "Maybe you can tell me where the nearest rest stop is."

"Better yet, I'll take you there." The officer smiled and nodded to Kara. "You help other people all the time. Now it's your turn to get a little assistance. Follow me." The officer turned to leave.

"Wait!" Kara cried out after the man. "How did you know that?"

The officer cocked his head and gave Kara a look that went straight to her soul. Almost as though the man knew everything about her. "We officers make it our business to know those things."

Kara glanced at Thane and saw that he was just as surprised as her. First the shoes, then the fact that she was tired. And finally the bit about her helping other people. All of it was right on, but how in the world had the officer known? She looked back at the man again. "Aren't you giving me a ticket or something?"

"Nope." Again the officer grinned. "Just wanted to make sure you were all right. That's my job, you know."

Kara nodded, distracted by the officer's strange

comments. The entire scene was like something from a sci-fi novel. And none of it made sense.

As soon as the patrolman was back in his car, he pulled out in front of Kara and motioned for her to follow. She did, staying behind him as he drove several miles south.

A minute later, Thane finally found his voice. "Kara, did you hear that guy?" Thane turned to face her. She could see without taking her gaze off the road that his face was ashen. "How did he know that stuff?"

"I'm not sure. It's weird, huh?"

"More than weird."

Intent on following the officer, Kara had no trouble staying awake. Finally the police car signaled and exited down a ramp off the interstate, where it made a quick right turn. Kara stayed as close behind as she could, taking the same turn. But at that point she could no longer see the police car. She hit the brake and stared straight ahead.

There was a rest area complete with a gas station and all-night restaurant and a parking lot. But the police car was nowhere. "Which way did he go?" She peered ahead and then glanced at Thane.

"He couldn't have gone far. We saw him turn this way and"—Thane looked out the window and scanned the parking lot—"there's nowhere else he could be."

"He must be in the parking lot." Kara continued into the rest area, driving slowly so she could find the police car. But her search turned up nothing. The police car was gone.

"Maybe he parked behind the restaurant." Thane sat back and studied Kara. "Where else could he be?"

Kara nodded. "You're right. That's probably it."

She parked near the front of the restaurant, and she and Thane climbed out of her car and waited. After five minutes, they walked around the perimeter of the restaurant, intent on finding the officer who had guided them to safety. Finally, they returned to the front of the restaurant and went inside.

"He must've taken a side road and gotten back on the freeway." Thane slid into a nearby booth and looked at Kara. "Police cars don't just disappear."

Suddenly Kara knew. She felt the hair on her arms rise straight up. "What if he was a . . . a . . ." Her mind raced with wonder. "An angel, Thane. I mean, how else could he have known that stuff?"

Kara and Thane called their parents and explained the situation. Kara's mother and father agreed to meet them at the rest stop, where one of them would drive the tired teens home. While they waited at the restaurant, the two talked more about the officer and whether he truly might have been an angel.

"He saved our lives, Thane. I was falling asleep when he came up behind me."

Together the teens decided there was only one way to find out. "His badge number was thirty-seven. Same number I wear in basketball. I saw it as clear as the look on his face." She took out her cell phone. "Let's call the police station and see who he is."

By calling information, Kara found the right number and waited while it rang. "I need to know the name of an officer," she said when someone answered. "He helped me and my friend out on the interstate a little while ago and I want to thank him."

"Badge number?"

"Three-seven." Kara waited, glad that in a few moments the mystery would be solved.

There was a pause. "Three-seven, that's all?"

"Yes." Kara's mouth felt dry. Come on, lady, tell me his name...

"Are you sure?"

"Yes," Kara said. "Positive."

"Well, you must not have caught a good look at the badge. You're missing a number." The woman's voice had taken on a strange tone. "We don't have any officers with that badge number. Nothing even close. Our officers have numbers with *three* digits."

The goose bumps were back. Kara hung up the phone and stared at Thane.

"What? Kara, don't do this to me. What'd they say?"

"It's true, Thane. He must've been an angel because their officers have three numbers on their badges. Not two."

There was a long moment where Thane said nothing. Then he took Kara's hands in his and said the thing she'd been praying he would say all year.

"I think it's time I made a decision about God." He kept his eyes on hers, his expression filled with awe. "I believe, Kara. I believe."

That very moment, the young couple bowed their heads and Kara prayed out loud. "Thank you, God, for sending an angel to us tonight. An angel in a police car. And thanks for making Thane believe." She hesitated, choking back the tears. "What happened tonight will stay with us as long as we live."

A Voice in the Storm

It looked like a great day for a winter hike. Kody Watts had no idea that in a few hours he'd be staring death in the face.

Kody Watts was eighteen that winter and pondering the same question all high school seniors face: What was he going to do after graduation? Never mind the snow and freezing temperatures—a hike would be the perfect chance to clear his head and consider his options.

His parents wanted him to stay close to home and attend nearby University of Michigan. If not there, then any college would do. So long as he enrolled somewhere. But Kody had other ideas. Tech school, maybe, or the Air Force. Something different and daring and adventurous. College could wait, couldn't it?

Just that morning he'd gotten into a fight with his parents over the issue.

"Son, we've prayed about your future since you

were a little boy." His mother put her hands on his shoulders and gave him her best sad look. "Listen to what God's telling you to do. Please."

Okay, fine. He would listen to God... if only he could hear him. God didn't just talk to people—at least not confused teenagers like himself.

Kody laced his hiking boots, slipped on a parka, and set out. His parents' home was near several large lakes and one was within walking distance. As he reached the frozen shore, he glanced at the horizon. Dark storm clouds were gathering in the northwest. Strange, he thought. There was no storm in the forecast. Not that he'd heard about, anyway.

Kody shrugged and zipped up his coat. He had a woolen hat and gloves and thermal underwear. He'd be fine. The clouds were too far off to worry about. But the breeze was stiffer than he'd expected. He buttoned the collar of his jacket tightly around his throat. There. That ought to do it.

The lake was large but fairly shallow. Each winter it froze over, creating a layer of ice strong enough for a truck to drive across. There were years when the very middle of the ice was a bit weak. But Kody didn't plan to go to the middle today. Just a nice purposeful hike around the perimeter. And three hours to think about his life.

What had happened to his boyhood plans, the ones he'd held on to even through middle school? He was going to be a doctor, wasn't he? An emergency room doctor, smack in the middle of chaos and confusion, life and death. Kody had figured he'd make a great doctor because he believed in the power of prayer. And that would certainly make a difference in an emergency room.

But sometime after his ninth-grade year, Kody had begun struggling with science and math.

"You better get with the program, Kode-ster," his older brother told him. "You'll take a lifetime of science and math before you get that medical degree you're after."

That had been the first time anyone had mentioned the idea that becoming a doctor might be hard. Not just hard, but next to impossible.

"You can do it, Kody," his father had told him at the end of that freshman year. "You apply yourself now and you'll have no trouble becoming a doctor. Don't give up your dream just because it won't be easy."

But then there'd been football and basketball and, well, girls. Lots of girls. He'd never gotten serious with any of them, but they took up time all the same. And the only way to afford the movies and dinner-dates was to work part time. All of which left precious little time for studying. Kody pulled C's and B's, but that was as good as it ever got.

Time passed and Kody kept walking.

At this point, University of Michigan wouldn't look at him. He'd have to start at a community college and work his way up. Kody exhaled hard and watched his breath form a foggy cloud just above his face. It was getting colder, no question about it. He gazed up and what he saw made his heart jump. The clouds had moved in over the lake and they looked ready to break loose at any moment.

He'd been walking nearly an hour now—some hundred yards off shore on the snow-covered ice. He wasn't quite halfway around the frozen lake, but there was no question he needed to turn around. If the storm broke he'd have to seek shelter somewhere. He hadn't even left a note for his parents. It was Saturday and they were both busy running errands. They thought he was home watching TV. If something happened to him, no one would have a clue where to find him.

The first snow began falling just as he turned around. *Okay, God, get me home safe.* He lowered his head and doubled his pace. There was no fear welling up within him. He'd been caught in storms before—just not this far from home. Besides, he always felt closer to God when he was outdoors like this. The Lord would be right beside him as he walked.

Minutes later, Kody stopped for a moment and surveyed the clouds once more. He was stunned by the change in the sky. Within minutes the clouds had grown dark and dangerously low, settling almost on top of the lake's frozen surface. Kody could feel the temperature dropping, and as he picked up his pace, the snow began falling harder. He looked to his left and realized he could no longer see the shore.

He kept his gaze straight ahead, but it was impossible to tell if he was walking the direction he wanted to or if he was heading out toward the center of the lake. All at once, a fierce wind came over him, bearing down on the ice and swirling the thick snow so that Kody could barely see his hand in front of his face.

It's a whiteout, God. Help me keep my direction.

He'd hoped to backtrack across the ice to the place where he'd started his hike. That way he'd have less trouble finding shelter and eventually making it home. But now Kody was afraid he might be heading toward the middle of the lake. If he did that there would be several problems. First, he could slip through the thin ice. A shudder ran down his spine. If that happened, he wouldn't have to worry about next year's plans. He would be in heaven before nightfall. But even if he didn't slip through the ice, he couldn't take the cold for very long without moving. And there was no way to know how long the storm would last.

That in mind, he changed his plan and turned left, moving toward what he hoped was the shore. Five minutes had passed since the blizzard had gotten serious. Instead of showing signs of letting up, it was growing more intense with each passing moment.

Kody walked for another ten minutes and figured he should be reaching the shore at any time. But five more minutes went by and another five, and a wave of panic made its way across Kody's heart. What if he wasn't heading toward shore? What if he'd gotten turned around so badly he didn't know where he was heading? By his guess the temperatures had dropped nearly thirty degrees since he'd set out on the hike. That meant it was below zero and colder with the wind chill. The air was burning his lips and throat, making his lungs ache. He brought his jacket up over his mouth and aimed his lips down, desperate for warmer air.

Maybe if I pick up my pace... Kody began jogging, but after another few minutes, he was winded and nearly out of energy. He hit a chunky section of ice and stumbled. As he struggled back to his feet, he realized something that scared him. Scared him more than anything ever had in all his life. He'd completely lost his sense of direction. He couldn't see even his hands now and he had no idea what direction to take.

A rush of dizziness swept over him and as he tried to move he fell again. What was this? Why had he lost his sense of balance? Then he realized what was happening. He was snow blind. It had happened back a few years ago to three local hikers in the woods during a storm. Rescue workers found two of their bodies and the third was unconscious for a month before he finally explained what had happened. They'd been caught in a whiteout, a blizzard. And they'd lost all sense of direction. Not just horizontal direction, but vertical direction as well.

Kody tried to stand up once more and again fell to the ice. Yes, that was it. That's exactly what was happening to him. He couldn't tell up from down because of the blinding snow. *God . . . I'm in trouble. Big trouble. Help me, Lord. Please, help me!*

In the years since he had first begun backpacking and exploring the forests near his home, Kody had read about people who had been trapped in sudden blizzards and become snow blind. The condition was a deadly one, because once it happened, a person could become completely disoriented and freeze to death, sometimes only inches from safety.

Kody pushed the thoughts from his mind and forced himself into a prone position on the ice. "I've got to keep moving," he ordered himself aloud. "Keep moving!"

Reaching forward, he dug his fingers into the snow and pulled his body along. The dizziness made him feel sick to his stomach. Now and then he would hear deep, powerful groans from beneath the lake's frozen surface.

"Help me!" he shouted. What if the ice cracked? Then he would drown in the freezing water for sure. "Help me! Somebody." But his cries for help were swallowed up in the wind. He grabbed another handful of snow and pulled himself forward again.

At least he could move.

Time passed and Kody was struck by another

frightening thought. What if he had been crawling in circles, wasting valuable energy and getting no closer to the shore? He stopped and dropped his head onto the snow and ice, closing his eyes to shut out the horrifying, blinding white that consumed him.

"Please, God, help me find my way!" He shouted the words as tears filled his eyes and froze on his cheeks.

At that moment, Kody heard the deep resonant sound of the foghorn, located at the rescue station at the edge of the lake, just blocks from his house. For the first time in nearly thirty minutes Kody had a reference point, a way to determine which way he was headed. Then he heard the sound of a voice speaking over the rescue station's private address system. "Be careful," the voice said clearly and loudly. "The ice has broken through at the middle of the lake. You're very close to that area."

Kody opened his eyes, his heart racing with hope. The storm was as strong as ever, the snow still a blinding, swirling white. But somehow the man at the rescue station had seen him. *Thank you, God. You heard my prayers.*

The man's words filled his head. *Be careful of the middle of the lake.* He must have wandered close to that point where the ice was broken. Kody drew a deep breath and began slithering toward the voice. Again he heard a warning. "Be careful. Stay to the right, and climb the concrete wall when you reach it."

The voice pushed Kody forward and filled him with peace. If he could continue toward the voice, eventually he'd reach the rescue station. Inch by inch, minute by minute, Kody kept on. He obeyed the voice, staying to the right. Finally, his hands numb and raw from pulling himself across the ice, he reached the wall. He looked up, exhausted. Peering through the storm, he saw the light from the rescue station ahead. He climbed over the retaining wall and felt his way through deep drifts of snow to the door of the rescue station.

"I'm alive," he whispered as he lifted his hand to knock. "I'm alive."

Before he could make contact with the wood, the door opened, and he could feel himself being pulled inside by a large man. Two minutes later, after Kody had caught his breath and could open his eyes, he looked into the warm, kind face of a bearded man he'd never seen before.

"Come on over here." The man helped Kody into a chair and offered him a mug of hot coffee.

"Thank you." Kody was too stunned to say anything else, though his heart was full. Instead, Kody stared at the man who had saved his life. Who was the guy? And how had he seen him through the blizzard well enough to guide him to safety? Whoever the man was, he was calm and peaceful; something about him put Kody immediately at ease.

The man was sitting at a table across the room and smiled at Kody. "You were lost out there." He stood to refill Kody's cup.

Kody nodded. "Yes, I didn't know where I was. Couldn't see anything."

The man looked intently at Kody. His eyes were crystal blue, a color Kody had never seen before. "Yes, I know. I knew you were lost so I sounded the foghorn. You were very close to the open water."

"How'd you know..." Kody licked his lips. They were still freezing cold. "I mean, how could you see me?"

"You asked for help." The man gave Kody a slight grin. "That's my job."

"Rescue worker, you mean?"

"You could say that." The man shrugged. "I needed to keep you safe out there."

As they were speaking, the weather cleared. Kody was still exhausted and needed to get home in case someone was worrying about him back home. "I better get going." He stood and shook the man's hand. "Thanks again. You...you saved my life."

As he was turning to leave, Kody remembered something. Normally the lake's rescue station was closed down for the winter. "Why were you here, anyway?"

"Doing research." The man winked at him.

Kody nodded, satisfied with the answer. He thanked the man again and walked home. Not until he was safely inside his parents' home did Kody realize he had been gone for seven hours. His parents were home and just about to call the police when Kody walked in.

They were at his side the moment he was through the door. It took Kody ten minutes to explain the entire story.

"That's impossible." His father crossed his arms and shook his head. "The station closes down in the winter."

"Maybe it was some other lakeside building," his mother offered.

Kody shook his head. "No, Mom, I know the rescue station. I've been going down to that lake forever." He sat on the nearest chair. "I know it's usually closed down by now, but this guy there really helped me. Said he was doing research or something."

His parents' eyebrows raised at the same time.

"The place has been closed down." His father's voice was gentle. "I went by there the other day. Closed for winter."

Frustration welled up in Kody. "Listen, I'm not losing my mind! I can still taste the coffee. The guy saved my life."

After a long night's sleep, Kody awoke the next morning determined to find the man at the rescue station and thank him again for saving his life. He dressed in his old blue parka and walked to the rescue building. As he approached the front door, Kody grew confused. The station was locked tightly, a chain through it's double doors. Its concrete-bunker design was lifeless and imposing. Puzzled, Kody made his way to the back door, but found it nearly buried under a three-foot-high snowdrift. It showed no signs of having been disturbed in weeks, if not months.

The image made no sense whatsoever. There had been no snow since the sudden storm the day before. The door should have shown obvious signs of Kody's tracks leading up and down the steps. Feeling more than a bit odd, Kody dug through the drift to the door and found a sign: "Closed for winter October to April."

Kody reminded himself to breathe. How could the station be closed? What had happened to his footprints leading up to the door? For that matter, where were the man's tracks? Kody studied the locked, snow-covered door again. How had the man gotten inside? He stood motionless, going over the details of the day before. This was definitely the place he had come to. This was where the man had poured him hot coffee and helped him off the lake. The only foghorn in the area was located here at the rescue station.

Suddenly, Kody knew there was one other way to check on the man's identity. The county sheriff's department ran the rescue station. Kody hurried home and placed a call to that office.

"No one's had access to the rescue station since

it was closed down in the fall. It's been completely vacant."

Kody hung up, his hands trembling. Maybe someone at the university would know what was going on. He placed another call and asked if anyone had been given permission to do research at the building.

"No." The voice sounded bored on the other end. "The county doesn't allow research at the rescue station during the off season."

Kody hung up the phone and fell to his knees, weak with the realization. Then he remembered the reason he'd gone on the hike in the first place—to search for direction. When it looked as though the storm might kill him, he'd begged God for direction again—a different kind of direction.

A hint of understanding washed over Kody.

"Could it have been?" Chills poked at his spine. "Is it possible?"

In that moment he realized it must have been and that yes, it was possible. God had worked out a miracle to save his life. And if God wanted his life saved, it must be so that he himself could go on to save the lives of others.

And that meant going to college to study medicine. Just like he used to dream of doing when he was younger.

Today Kody is at medical school, well on his way to becoming a doctor. And though he can't prove it, he's convinced that the man who saved his life that terrible winter day was none other than an angel. An angel sent to show him the way home . . . and the way to a future that God had planned for him all along.

Missing Daddy

Tina Ewing had always been close to her father. When she was a little girl growing up in Boston, Paul Ewing would come home from work and spend hours pretending to be the horse while Tina bounced on his back.

As Tina moved into middle school, the two continued to share a special bond. Tina became a talented soccer player and was chosen for an advanced-level all-star team. The girls played in tournaments across the state and every weekend Tina's father would accompany her, cheering words of encouragement to Tina as she played her heart out.

When Tina made the decision to give up soccer during her sophomore year, it was her father who was most supportive. "You've done your best, sweetheart." He kissed the top of her head. "Maybe it's time to try something else."

Tina's mother was an executive at a local bank and she kept long hours. Her father was self-employed and could work his schedule around Tina's activities. When she got involved in volleyball and basketball that year, he was at every game. When Tina's mother worked weekends, Tina and her father would go sailing or roller-blading. Those were the afternoons when Tina's father would tell her that God had plans for her life—great plans.

"Never doubt for a minute how much God loves you." He'd grin at her. "Get that part right and everything in life will fall into place."

That year, during an essay contest, Tina's teacher asked her to name and describe her best friend. "My dad's my best friend," she wrote. "He understands me better than anyone else."

Tina was only eighteen when her father began losing weight and coughing. It took three months for a doctor to give the family the diagnosis they were dreading. Tina's father had lung cancer. Worse, it had spread to his liver. Two months later he was hospitalized and called Tina to his bedside.

"Don't blame...God for this, sweetheart." He managed a smile, though he was breathless from the effort of talking. "God's calling me home, but your mother and I are at peace. It's part of his plan, for whatever reason."

Tina held back her tears, then and when he died two weeks later. It wasn't until after his funeral service that she broke down and wept. Her mother found her in her room and sat on the bed beside her. "He'll always be with you, baby. Always."

But for months, Tina couldn't shake the dark cloud his absence had left. There were times when she'd go to school and spend the day in the library, missing every class. Calls to her mother did nothing to help.

"I can't make myself think, Mom. I miss him so much."

Her mother took time off from work to take Tina to counseling sessions, but nothing seemed to help. She lost weight and dark circles appeared beneath her once-bright eyes.

"Your father would be heartbroken, dear," her mother told her one day. "I'm praying for you. And somewhere I know your father is praying, too."

Her mother's words rang in Tina's head. It was true, of course. Prayer, divine intervention, God's miraculous power was the only way she would survive. But where was she supposed to start? How did she begin a conversation with God when he was the very one who had let her father die?

They were thoughts Tina hated to have, but they were there all the same. And as the months passed, there was an emptiness inside her that she could neither escape nor explain. She barely graduated from high school and spent the summer moping about the house. Then, that fall, sometime near the anniversary of her father's death, Tina and two of her friends, Diane and Lora, decided to hike along a lake that had been one of her father's favorites.

"I'm not sure we should be doing this." The hole in Tina's heart felt bigger than the lake in front of them as she and the others got out of the car and headed toward the water. Parts of the hike would be hilly, and Tina didn't have the energy to climb them. And what about the memories along the way? Every step of this hike would remind her of her father.

"Come on, Tina. It's time." Diane gently pulled Tina's arm and led her toward the trail.

Tina closed her eyes. *God . . . give me the strength.* When she blinked them open, she felt a little more capable than before. "I know." She inhaled slowly. "Now or never."

The three friends headed toward the lake. For nearly thirty minutes, the threesome walked in silence, each lost in her own thoughts. They rounded a corner and Tina remembered the time she and her father had stopped in that spot when she twisted her ankle once.

"Can you make it, honey?" She could still hear her father's voice, caring for her, encouraging her.

One after another the memories of her father bombarded her with an almost physical force. The three friends turned a corner to approach the steepest hill of the climb. The path followed the hill straight up and then leveled off along a fifty-yard plateau. At the top of the hill, a bench marked the spot where Tina and her father had often sat and talked when they visited the lake. Tina swallowed hard and stared straight ahead. She would have to take the hill by storm, facing every memory along the way and refusing to give in to her overwhelming feelings of grief.

Then suddenly she saw someone on the hill high above her.

A tall man in jeans and a T-shirt stood on the plateau staring out at the lake. From her viewpoint, the man looked exactly like her dead father. Tina gasped, but her friends didn't seem to hear her. The trio continued up the hill. As they did, Tina kept her eyes on the man, and suddenly she felt a burden being lifted from her shoulders. When they were just ten yards from the man, he turned toward Tina and smiled the same warm and reassuring smile that had once belonged to Paul Ewing alone.

Tina's friends still seemed oblivious to the man and continued past him without stopping. When Tina was only a few feet away from him, she paused and stared into his eyes. He winked once, smiled again, and then slowly turned back toward the lake.

Although Tina did not believe that people could come back from the dead or that people became angels after death, at that instant, she had no doubt that somehow this man was her father. She did not know how it could be possible, but there was no way anyone could look so much like him and be anyone else. She seemed to know, instinctively, that there was no need to question the man or engage in dialogue. A peaceful reassurance washed over her. She smiled at the man one last time and nodded as she continued on her way. At the bottom of the hill, she caught up with her friends and asked them to stop a moment.

"Did you see that man?" She could feel the way her eyes were shining. Something they hadn't done since her father had died. Finally, after months of grieving, she felt at peace with herself.

"What man?" Diane's expression was blank.

"Yeah, who?" Lora tilted her head, her eyebrows lowered.

"You know who." Tina cocked her head curiously. "That man, up on the top of the hill." She pointed toward the hill, but the man had vanished. "He was up there, near the bench."

Diane looked at Lora and shrugged. "I didn't see anyone, did you?"

"Not a person. We've been the only ones on the trail all day."

"No, seriously, guys. Back there on the hill. That guy in the jeans. He looked just like my—"

Tina stopped short. Her friends would think she was crazy if she finished her sentence. Besides, if they hadn't seen anyone, then... Tina felt another wave of peace. There was no need to share the story of the man and her meeting with him.

"Never mind." Tina began walking again. "Must've been my imagination."

Diane and Lora shrugged; Tina was thankful when they dropped the subject. Whoever the man was, he had given her a glimpse of the father she so badly missed and the reassurance that she had desperately needed. She would keep the incident to herself for a while and savor it. And regardless of what anyone else would say to doubt it, from that point on Tina was convinced that an angel, somehow cloaked in the appearance of her father, had been there. Perhaps he would always be there, watching over the daughter Paul Ewing had loved so much.

This notion was confirmed five years later when Tina was working in Los Angeles near the Federal Building. She went into town for lunch and was returning back to work when she paused at the curb, waiting for the light to change.

Suddenly, there was a firm grasp of a hand on her shoulder. The hand pulled her away from the curb with a force so strong it nearly knocked her to the ground. At the exact same instant, a city bus jumped the curb directly where Tina had been standing. If she had remained standing there, she'd have been killed.

She turned at once to thank the person who had rescued her, but there was no one within fifty feet of her. Again she felt an overwhelming sense of peace and reassurance.

"The Bible says God assigns his angels to watch over us," Tina says now. "He did that for me when I was a teenager, devastated by my father's death. And he does it still."

A Face Like Jesus

The market colors began changing while Steve Getz was shopping for a cold can of Mountain Dew. Mixed up with the wrong crowd during his eighth grade year, Steve had dabbled with drugs ever since. But that summer he had just turned sixteen and promised his parents he was finished with doing drugs and hanging out with other people who did them.

But in the San Francisco neighborhood where he lived, drugs were easy to find and the shady friends hard to shake. Less than a month after his birthday he began using again and now here he was on a full-blown trip like he'd never experienced before. An hour before coming to the market, Steve had taken a mixture of illegal drugs, and now, suddenly, the walls of the market seemed to be melting, their colors running into each other.

Without a doubt Steve hated this—hated how it made him feel panicked and sweaty, hated how his heart raced, making him feel like he wouldn't last another minute. Steve looked around desperately, trying to steady himself, aware that sweat had begun pouring from his forehead, dripping down his face, neck, and arms. *Why do I do this to myself?* The thought tapped at the inside of his brain until the sound became a deafening drumbeat.

"Not now," he whispered out loud. "Please not now."

He turned toward the produce section, but the fruit and vegetables had turned into large blob-like substances, and worse, they were coming toward him.

"Help!" he screamed. Then he began running full speed through the store, up one aisle and down the next. Finally, alerted by concerned customers, the store manager and someone who looked like a customer caught Steve and forced him to the ground. As strange as Steve was feeling he was surprised at the strength of the customer, a tall man Steve guessed to be in his late twenties.

"Hold his feet!" The customer directed the store manager toward Steve's legs. "I've got his arms."

Steve could barely make sense of any of it. His heart was fluttering within him and he couldn't breathe right. He struggled to break free from the grasp of the two men, but he couldn't find the strength. The hallucinations were worse than ever and he felt himself twist wildly on the floor. He had to be free! The tomatoes were going to get him, bury him alive if he didn't find a way out.

Steve closed his eyes but when he opened them, he screamed in terror at what he saw. Horrible, dark demons were coming toward him. They had fierce expressions and fangs that dripped blood. There were small, evil demons floating near his face and laughing at him, and there were huge, monstrous demons circling him. Worse than the way they looked, the demons seemed to be emanating a sense of utter evil, a death and destruction that Steve was powerless to escape.

"Help me! Someone help me," he shouted. "They're trying to kill me."

The customer, who had been holding Steve's arms, leaned in closer to him.

"You're going to be okay." The man's voice was soothing and clear. Despite Steve's severe hallucinations, he could hear the man, and he began nodding.

"Help me!" he shouted again.

"Open your eyes, Steve." The customer's voice was calm, and no one else around them seemed to hear it. Steve kept his eyes closed. He could hear a crowd of people gathering around them, but he tuned them out. With all the concentration he could muster, he forced himself to listen to the man. "Come on, Steve, you can trust me."

Steve opened his eyes slowly. As the picture became clearer, his eyes grew wide in astonishment. The demons were still there, but they were retreating. And in the center of the picture was what appeared to be the face of Jesus Christ. Steve was sure that's who the guy looked like. After all, his parents had taken him to church when he was a kid. It was the same picture of Jesus he'd had in his Bible storybook back then. Awestruck, Steve stopped twisting and struggling and suddenly grew calm.

As he stared, the image in the center of the picture began to speak. "Do you want to be free from the demons, Steve?" the voice of the Christlike image asked. "You need to decide."

Suddenly, Steve began to cry. The crowd, which had grown even larger, watched as the young man continued to lean over him, talking in a voice none of them could hear.

"Yes," Steve cried softly. He thought of his parents back home and all the bad decisions he'd made. He needed to be free from the drugs. Now, before it was too late. He struggled to find his voice. "Help me get rid of the demons. Please help me!" The man in the picture smiled gently. "No more drugs, Steve. With them come the demons. It is your choice."

"No, I can't do it by myself!" Steve screamed. The customer stayed at his side, uttering calm words—words different from the ones uttered by the Christlike image, but somehow words that seemed to go together. Steve closed his eyes again and once more started to struggle out of the stranger's grasp. But the man seemed to possess an inhuman strength and Steve's efforts were futile.

"Look at me, Steve," the gentle voice said again. "Trust me."

Slowly, Steve opened his eyes again. This time the demons were gone completely. Only the image of a very pure and radiant Christ filled the center of his vision.

"Help me." Steve's voice was weak now, and tears filled his eyes. "Please."

"Steve, you won't have to do this by yourself. If you want to be rid of the demons, turn to me. I will always be right here to help you. Just call me and I will be with you."

"Lord." Steve whispered the word, not sure if he was still hallucinating, but savoring the peace he felt all the same. *Is that you, God? Are you really here, with me, talking to me?*

Slowly the image began to fade. But before it disappeared altogether, he heard the voice once more. "Yes, Steve. It is I. I will be here for you."

Suddenly Steve felt extremely tired. He closed his eyes and his body went limp.

The customer who had been talking quietly to Steve and holding down his arms stood up and turned to the manager. "I think you can handle it from here." He shook the man's hand. "The worst of it's over."

"Thanks." The manager looked a little awed at the customer's strength and ability to calm down the drugged teenager. Before he said anything more, the manager pinned down Steve's arms in case he woke up again. When the manager looked around to ask the customer how he'd managed to calm the drugged teen, the man had vanished. At that moment, paramedics and police arrived and the manager stepped back so they could work on the boy.

"Excuse me," a woman said as she made her way to the teenager. "I'm his mother. Please let me see him."

Steve's mom, a pretty, dark-haired woman with tears in her eyes, moved next to Steve and watched as paramedics took his vital signs. A friend of Steve's had called and told her that he had taken a lot of drugs.

"I'm worried about him, Mrs. Getz. He went to the market, but he's in no shape to drive."

She had raced to the store, terrified she'd find his car crashed on the road somewhere along the way. Now she stood back so some paramedics could work on her son. "Is he... is he going to live?"

"Seems to be okay now," one of them said. "Drug hallucination?" The paramedic directed the question to the store manager.

"Yes, definitely. Never seen anything like it."

Steve's mother closed her eyes and let the tears come. Steve had promised her his days of doing drugs were behind him. He had been in and out of a rehabilitation center twice since his thirteenth birthday, and now this. Would he ever quit? Would she forever be hunting him down, worrying about whether he was killing himself or someone else because of his drug addiction? She and her husband prayed for him every day, but Steve hadn't believed in God since he was young. Where would he ever find the strength to leave the drugs and partying if he didn't grab hold of the faith he'd once had?

The paramedics backed away from Steve. "He needs a place to sober up, but there's nothing wrong with him medically." They nodded to Steve's mother. "I'm sorry about this, ma'am. It must be very difficult."

She nodded and bit her lower lip. Tears would serve no purpose now. She needed to figure out a way to get Steve home. After that, she and her husband could figure out what the next step was. She moved in close to Steve's head.

"Steve . . . wake up," she whispered. When he was asleep like this—even lying prone on the floor of a supermarket—he still looked like the kindhearted child he'd once been. Her heart grieved at all he'd lost, all he'd become over the years. "Come on, Son, get up."

Steve opened his eyes. It took only seconds for the frantic confusion she'd seen so often to flash across his face. "Where is he?" He glanced around the circle of people still gathered near him. Then he looked at his mother. "Mom, where did he go?"

Great, more hallucinations. A wave of embarrassment washed over her and she kept her voice low. "I don't know who you're talking about, Steve."

Steve sat straight up and looked around until he

saw the store manager. "Where did he go, that man who was holding me down?"

The manager glanced at the crowd, which had dwindled to just a few people. "I guess he's gone."

Slowly, Steve rose to his feet, his arms and legs shaking. The strange images were gone, but there was no question the drugs were still working their way through his body. At that instant, a policeman moved in and placed handcuffs on Steve's wrists as he read him his rights.

"Wait a minute!" Steve's mother stepped back, her eyes wide. "Why are you arresting him? I'll take him home and he'll be fine there. Please . . . don't do this."

One of the officers cast her a kind glance. "His hallucination took place in a public market, ma'am. We're arresting him for making a public disturbance."

The other officer nodded his agreement. "Besides, it'll be hours before he's sober again. There's some concern he could act wild again. We want him in handcuffs for his safety as well as that of the people around him."

Before the police led him away, Steve turned again to the manager. "Please . . ." He was suddenly much calmer than he had been moments earlier. "Tell me what that man looked like, the man who talked to me."

The manager squirmed uncomfortably at the strange request. "He was . . . well," he began, trying to remember. "He was a customer. He had short blond hair, a muscular build and, let's see, well, a real clean-shaven face. That's all I can remember."

Steve shook his head. "No, I mean the other man. The one who leaned over me and talked to me."

The manager frowned. "Yes, that's who I'm telling you about."

Steve shook his head, desperate to know about the other man. The one who'd looked like Christ. "No, the man who helped me. He had dark hair, a beard, brown eyes. Where is he?"

The manager stared at him, his face blank. At that point, his mother stepped in and placed her hand on Steve's arm. "Maybe it was the drugs, Son."

"No, Mom, it was a man. I saw him right above me, looking at me, talking to me. He even knew my name."

The manager drew a slow breath. "All I can tell you is that the man who helped you was a blond guy."

The police were anxious to leave, but Steve's mother stopped as though she'd suddenly remembered something. She looked at the manager. "You're sure the man who helped my son was blond?"

"Definitely." The manager shrugged. "He left right after your son calmed down."

The police led Steve toward the door. "We need to take him to the station now." They nodded toward Steve's mother. "You're welcome to follow us."

As they walked toward the front of the store, Steve looked back at his mother. His face was paler than before. "Something happened in there." He shook his head. "My life will never be the same again, Mom."

He saw the frightened look on her face, unsure of what to make of his statement.

"Don't worry." He smiled as tears built in his eyes. "I'll tell you everything later."

Steve was booked and released from the police station after promising to appear in court to deal with his public disturbance charge. His mother took him home a few hours later. Normally after he'd gotten into trouble because of his drug use, Steve was angry and defiant. But as he approached his mother in their car and climbed inside, he was strangely upbeat.

"Okay, what is it Steve? What happened back there at the store?" His mother leaned back in the driver's seat, waiting for Steve to explain himself.

"It was the strangest thing. Not like my other drug trips, Mom. I'm serious."

"What you saw was strange?"

"At first it was like usual—vegetables chasing me, that kind of thing. But then this man looked at me. His face was..." Steve stopped himself. "Mom, do you think God might be trying to tell me something?"

His mother swallowed. Steve hadn't talked about God in years. "Of course, Son. That's what your dad and I pray for every day. That God will get through to you, whatever it takes." She hesitated. "So finish your story. What happened back there?"

Steve told the story, careful not to miss any details.

He drew a shaky breath. "I began sweating and then I think I started running through the store screaming for help." His eyes narrowed, ashamed at himself for how he'd acted, thankful his mother hadn't seen the worst of it. "Then I began seeing black little beings in the air and I closed my eyes. I think I just stood there screaming for help. When I opened my eyes, there were demons; that's the only way I can describe them. They were all around me... black beings with fangs and claws and blood dripping from their mouths. Oh, Mom, it was so horrible."

Steve hung his head for a moment, reliving the nightmare of the hallucination. His mother reached over and took his hand.

"What happened next?"

Steve wiped at a stray tear on his cheek. "I felt someone grab me and take hold of my feet. Someone else was holding my arms. I had my eyes closed and I was still screaming. Then, all of a sudden I could hear this calm, gentle voice telling me to open my eyes and to trust him. Now, here's where it gets really weird. I opened my eyes slowly and the demons were leaving; they were moving away as fast as they could. And in the middle of the image was a man who looked exactly like the pictures of Jesus. You know, pictures from my Sunday school class as a kid. Anyway, he was holding my arms real gentle, speaking soft so that only I could hear him."

"What did he say?" His mother looked like she was hanging on every word.

"He told me that if I wanted to get rid of the demons I would have to stop the drugs. Then he told me he would help me so I wouldn't have to do it on my own."

His mother lifted her hand to her mouth. "Steve . . . that's amazing."

"After that I felt a lot of peace. The demons had gone completely, and I sort of fell asleep for a few moments. When I woke up, I wanted to talk to the man. But he was gone. No one knew where he was."

"Is it the same man the manager says was blond?"

"I guess so. Everyone must have seen him. There were lots of people standing around when all this was happening."

"And no one saw where he went?"

"No." Steve blinked, grateful that the drugs were wearing off. "But you want to know what's the weirdest thing of all?"

His mother nodded.

"I know that guy was sent by God to warn me. If I don't accept God's help now and change my life, the demons will get me. I believe that's why he appeared to me like that."

"But what about the blond guy? Was he talking to you or was it some image in your hallucination?"

"I'm not sure. But everyone saw the man who held me down talking to me. They just couldn't hear what he was saying."

"So you think it was a warning?" His mother's voice was lighter, her expression more relaxed. "Son, I've prayed that your life would change, but I never expected this type of answer from the Lord."

Steve studied his mom, his heart overflowing with resolve. "I'll never touch drugs again, Mom. I'm going to turn to God and give him back his place in my life. I don't want what happened today to be for nothing."

"Hmmm," his mother tilted her head. "It's interesting."

"What?"

"It's a miracle, I guess. You were given a message from God the same way people used to get them back in biblical times."

Steve was confused. "Really?"

"From angels, Steve." A glow spread across her face. "Maybe the man who talked to you was an angel, telling you what the Lord wanted you to hear."

Steve thought a moment. "I guess I'll never know. But it's going to change my life, Mom. I promise you that."

Steve made several follow-up phone calls to the supermarket in search of the man who had helped him that afternoon. But the manager apparently never saw the man again. Whoever he was, he'd been available, he'd helped in an emergency situation, and then disappeared.

But not in vain.

Steve kept his word. For the next twenty years and still today, Steve Getz has stayed away from all drugs. He has also maintained a dynamic relationship with God, one that began on a cold, supermarket floor in the grasp of a man who was, perhaps, an angel.

A Warning from Heaven

Laughter had always been the glue that held together the friendship between Donna West and Vicki Cutter. They met in first grade and though they had their disagreements they always found something to smile about. Something that only made their friendship stronger through the years.

"You two are more like sisters than friends," their mothers often told them.

It was true. And never more so than the summer of their fifteenth year. The girls were excited about starting their sophomore year at a Phoenix high school close to their homes. Every day since school let out they'd been inseparable. They took turns spending the night at each other's houses. And three times they'd spent the day with friends at a local water park. But one of their favorite ways to spend the days was by hanging out at Donna's aunt's house. Aunt Kerry was only twenty-four and married to a great guy. The couple lived just a block away from Donna and their backyard contained one of the nicest pools in the neighborhood.

Besides that, there was something different about Kerry. She and her husband believed in God and even talked about him in everyday conversations. Not just at Easter and Christmas like Donna's parents or Vicki's. But after a morning swim or between stores at the shopping mall.

Donna was sure about what made Aunt Kerry different, and someday—when she was older—she hoped to have that same kind of faith. She told Vicki as much that July day as they made their way down the street toward Kerry's house.

"Whatever she's got, I want it." Donna kicked at a loose bit of gravel as they walked. "I just don't know if I want it now."

Vicki thought about that for a moment. "What was it your aunt told us the other day? Something about Young Life?"

"Right." Donna tilted her head up and gazed at the clear blue sky. The day was going to be a scorcher, well over a hundred degrees. "It's a club that meets at school. Maybe we should check it out when school starts up again."

They walked a bit more and Kerry greeted them at the front door. "Hey!" She smiled at them both. Her purse was over her shoulder and she held her car keys in her hands. "I was just going to the store." She pointed back at the house. "Three burned-out lightbulbs and not a new one in the house."

"Oh." Donna felt a ripple of disappointment. "That's okay. We were just gonna hang out and swim for a while."

Aunt Kerry bit her lip. Then her eyes lit up. "Why don't you come with me. We can swim when we get back."

Donna and Vicki looked at each other and shrugged. It didn't matter if it was a routine errand. With Aunt Kerry the outing was bound to be fun. And funny. Kerry had a great sense of humor and appreciated the silliness that was a trademark of Donna and Vicki's friendship.

Donna grinned. "You sure you don't mind?"

"Not at all." Kerry slipped out onto the porch, shut the front door of her house, and locked it. "We'll be real quick, I promise."

On the way to the store, Vicki told a funny story about a baseball game the day before. "All our friends are on this summer team, so we thought we should go." She paused. "You know . . . to support them. So we're sitting in the bleachers and the game's about half over when Donna stands up, walks over to the dugout, and nudges one of the guys through the fence and asks them about halftime."

"I thought we'd missed it." Donna's voice was half whine, half giggle. "No one ever told me baseball doesn't have a halftime."

Aunt Kerry laughed from the front seat. "You girls are so goofy. Both of you."

Donna and Vicki barely paused before telling

Kerry another story. By the time they reached the store, the three of them were breathless from laughing so hard. Aunt Kerry pulled in and parked the car. "You girls want to stay here or come in with me?"

The parking place was in the shade just a few spots down the center row of parking. It would be cool and probably more fun than going inside. Besides, it wasn't quite ten in the morning yet. Donna spoke up first. "We'll stay here. Besides," she cast a quick grin at Vicki. "I haven't told Vicki what Kyle said about her yet."

"What?" Vicki leaned forward, her eyes wide. "I've been with you for an hour already! I didn't even know you'd talked to Kyle."

Aunt Kerry smiled. "Sounds like you girls have a lot to catch up on." She rolled down all the windows, climbed out, and shut the door. "I'll be right back."

Not three minutes later, after the story about Kyle was finished, Donna's eyes lit up. "Hey…I have an idea."

Vicki was immediately in agreement. "What?"

"Let's play a trick on Aunt Kerry."

"Aunt Kerry?" Vicki's eyes clouded some. "But Donna…she's always so nice to us."

"Not a mean trick." Donna gave Vicki a light push. "Just something to make her laugh."

"Like what?"

And with that, Donna began to explain the plan.

* * *

Less than ten minutes passed before Kerry Miller left the store and headed for her car. Almost immediately she noticed something was wrong. The girls were no longer in the car. She held back a sigh as she slid her package onto the front passenger seat and climbed behind the wheel. As funny as Donna and Vicki were, sometimes they didn't know when to draw the line. They'd played tricks on Kerry before, and usually the jokes were funny—pretending to drop an ice cube down her back or splashing her when they were in the pool. But this . . . this disappearance was definitely not funny. She peered out the side window, searching for any sign of them. "Donna! Vicki!" Kerry yelled their names and waited. When there was no response, she tried again. "Girls . . . I'm leaving. This isn't funny."

God, where are they? Kerry scanned the sidewalk in front of the store once more. Had they gotten hot and gone inside? Or were they in another store along the strip mall? Panic rattled the windows of Kerry's heart. What if it wasn't a joke? What if something had happened to them?

In that instant, Kerry got an idea. She would leave the parking lot and head straight for the police station. That way if something had happened to them, the officers could begin the search more quickly. And if not, when the girls saw her car leaving the area, they were bound to come running from one of the stores.

Kerry slipped the key into the ignition and

revved up the engine. She put the car into first gear, and since there were no cars parked in front of her, she started to drive straight ahead. Once she caught the girls' attention, she could circle back and pick them up. *Then I'll be honest with them*, she told herself. *This kind of thing isn't funny. Help me find them, God.*

Then, just as Kerry moved her foot off the brake and onto the gas pedal, she heard a distinct voice from the back of the car.

"Back up!" The voice was deep, with a sort of intensity Kerry hadn't heard before. "Go backwards!" Without hesitating, Kerry obeyed, not knowing why or who had spoken the words. It didn't matter who spoke them, because the power and authority in the voice was beyond doubting. She had backed up five feet when she saw them.

Donna and Vicki, crouched in front of Kerry's car, low and giggling. They had been hiding by the front grill of the car the entire time. Nausea rushed across Kerry's gut and she felt her body grow weak. Had she sped forward as she'd planned, she would have run over the girls and probably killed them both.

Unaware of the danger they had been in, the girls came giggling toward the car and climbed inside. "Tricked you, didn't we?" Donna's smile showed she had no clue what kind of disaster they'd just been spared.

Kerry slipped the car into park once again and turned around. She was shaking. "That wasn't funny, girls. I thought you were going to stay in the car until I got back."

The girls' faces fell. "Sorry," Donna said softly. "We were just trying to have fun with you."

Aunt Kerry was silent the rest of the way home, choosing not to tell the girls about what had nearly happened until they pulled in the driveway. Then she explained how she was going to pull forward.

"But a voice stopped me. An audible voice told me to back up instead."

"Wow." Donna felt more than a little guilty. The whole idea seemed ridiculous now that it had turned into a problem. The last thing she wanted to do was upset Aunt Kerry. "A real voice?"

"Sure sounded like it."

"Would... would we have died, Aunt Kerry?"

Kerry was quiet for a moment. "I think so. My car would've knocked you down and then crushed you."

"But how can someone talk to you if no one's there?"

"Well... I'd say it was a miracle." Kerry settled back against the seat of her car and for the first time she explained her faith to the girls. "I have a relationship with God, not just a religion." Kerry's heartbeat was finally back to normal. "Is that something you'd like to know more about?"

Both girls nodded their heads. And for the first time that summer, the story Kerry shared with them wasn't merely something to make them laugh. It was the truth about her faith in God and how Donna and Vicki could have the same faith.

Before the day was up, both girls made the most serious decision of their lives by praying with Kerry. Not just thanking God for the miraculous voice that saved their lives, but asking him to be in their lives the way he was in Aunt Kerry's.

The Sweetest Friend

Tami Bolton's father needed just two words to turn her entire life upside down.

"We're moving!" he announced one day. Then he went on to explain that he'd found a job in Southern California where he could concentrate on his career in solar energy.

Tami had known this day might come. She had known it since her father had first brought the idea up the year before. But at sixteen she wasn't ready to leave Missouri, especially two thousand miles away from her married sister and friends in the Midwest.

"I can't move." Tears welled up in her eyes and she hugged herself. "Everyone I know is here, Daddy. Can't you wait another year? Until I'm ready to live on my own?"

Her father's expression softened. "I'd like to stay, too, Tami. Your mom and I know how hard this'll be for you, for all of us. But this is the job I've been waiting years to get. I don't have any choice, honey."

He gave her shoulder a gentle squeeze. "Besides, you can move back after you finish high school. Maybe get a dorm and go to school here. That's only a few years away."

Tami nodded but she couldn't speak. If she did, an ocean of tears would come at the same time. Instead she managed a sad smile and headed upstairs to her room. There she threw herself on her bed and buried her face in the pillow. How could they do this to her? Move her away from her friends when she was about to start her junior year in high school? Nothing would be the same in California. She'd miss all the milestones she and her friends had planned on. Prom, graduation, applying for college admission together.

God, can't you change his mind? Make my dad understand that this isn't the best thing for us. Please, God.

Within the hour, her mother entered her room and sat on the side of her bed. "Tami, I'm sorry you're upset."

Tami rolled over onto her back and studied her mother through swollen eyes. "Is he serious? We're really moving to California?"

Her mother nodded. "It's a great opportunity for him, honey. It might only last a few years. Then we could all move back." She brushed back Tami's bangs with her fingertips. "We have to believe God will bring us back here sometime. This is home. Not just for you, sweetheart. For all of us."

Another wave of tears fell from Tami's eyes and

she sniffed, searching for her voice. "I can't even imagine telling my friends good-bye after so many years. And what about Mari?"

Mari Bolton Rice was six years older than Tami but the two sisters had always shared a special bond. Last year when Mari married her high school sweetheart, Tami was her maid of honor.

Tami watched her mother's expression fall. "We'll all miss Mari. But we'll visit. I can promise you that much, honey."

For a long while they stayed there, Tami and her mother, each appreciating the fact that they faced the pain of moving together. Finally, when Tami had a better grip on her emotions, she reached out and took hold of her mother's hand. "At least I'll have you and Misty."

Her mom's body stiffened at the mention of Tami's cat. "Now, honey, that's something we need to talk about."

"What?" Tami sniffed, wiping her cheeks with her fingertips.

"About Misty." She paused. "Your father and I talked about it, and, well, there's no way we can bring her. We're flying to California and once we get there, we'll rent an apartment. Mari's offered to take her. I think that's a much better answer for Misty, dear."

"Mom, you can't be serious." Tami raised her voice. Misty had slept on the end of her bed since she was eight years old. Sometimes at night after

Tami was done talking to God, she would share her heart with the old gray cat. Again fresh tears stung at Tami's eyes. "Misty's part of the family. She has to come."

"Tami, be sensible." Her mother kept her voice calm, gentle. "Can you imagine what type of life Misty would have in an apartment? Here she spends the days chasing mice in the field behind our house. She knows her way around. It'd be the same thing with all the space at Mari's house. But an apartment?" Her mother kissed her on the cheek, then stood to leave. "Please, Tami. Try to understand."

But after her mother left the room, Tami spent an hour crying in her room. She couldn't understand any of it. Not the move, not the idea of leaving her friends and her sister, and certainly not the idea of leaving Misty.

But over the next few weeks, Tami had no choice but to give in to the idea. Her mother was right; it would be cruel to confine Misty to an apartment all day. Especially when the three of them would be gone at school and work. What kind of a life would that be for an old cat? Finally, even as she felt her world crumbling around her, Tami knew that giving the cat to Mari was the only answer.

When moving day arrived three months later, Tami placed Misty in her sister's arms. "Here." She was sobbing, weary from all the good-byes she'd said that week. "Take good care of her, okay?"

"I will, sweetie." Her sister hugged her close, the cat between them. "I'll miss you so much, Tami."

"Me, too." Tami buried her head in her sister's shoulder. "How am I going to make it, Mari?"

"You'll make it. The weeks will pass quickly." Mari pulled away and sniffed twice. "Before you know it you'll be back again."

The flight across the country was quiet and somber, with Tami lost in thoughts of all she'd left behind. Her parents were serious, but excited all the same. Halfway to California they became caught up in a conversation about her father's new job.

Easy for you both, Tami thought as she looked out the window. But what about me? She stared as far up as she could see. *What about me, God, huh? Can you see my heart breaking?*

When they arrived, the Boltons found a small, two-bedroom apartment not far from where Tami's father would be working. Soon afterward they joined a church in the area, and Tami decided to have a positive attitude.

But as the weeks passed she grew more homesick, constantly thinking of her friends and her sister and her precious feline friend, Misty. Many afternoons she would come home from her new school, lay on her bed, and wish for a way to turn back the clock. Her attitude was affecting the atmosphere of their small home, and Tami was sorry about that. Normally the Bolton household was filled with fun and laughter. But Tami couldn't seem to shake the feeling of isolation.

Two months passed and her parents bought a beautiful home with a swimming pool, but even that didn't help. Worst of all, she felt far from God, almost as if he were unaware of her situation, unable to help her feel better.

"I'm sorry I've been so sad lately," she told her parents a month later. "I don't want to spoil things for you guys." She shot a weak smile toward her father. "I know you're excited about your new job and the house, and I'm happy for you. Really. It's just that sometimes I feel so lonely it's almost like I'm suffocating."

Later that night, Tami's parents thought about her apology and the way she'd tried to adjust to their new home. "Tami's birthday is next week, right?" Tami's father sat back in his chair, his eyes twinkling.

"Yes." Her mother sighed. "I've been trying to think of a way to cheer her up, but there doesn't seem to be much we can do."

Tami's father smiled. "I think I just thought of a way."

The next week, on Tami's birthday, the two of them presented Tami with a tiny gray kitten.

"Oh my goodness," she squealed, taking the tiny ball of fur into her arms. "He's perfect. Thank you so much."

For the first time since their move Tami looked

genuinely happy, and her parents congratulated themselves on finding the perfect birthday present for her.

"He'll have to be a house cat." Her father came up to her and stroked the kitten's soft gray fur. "He won't have acres of fields to play in, but he won't know any different."

"Happy birthday, honey." Tami's mother slipped an arm around her shoulder. "Maybe now you won't be so lonely."

Tami named the kitten Chloe, and with a new friend to keep her company, her outlook changed overnight. She began meeting more kids at school and took a greater interest in her classes. Then she would hurry home to share the afternoon with Chloe.

Over the next few months, she spent hours playing with the kitten, training her, and teaching her the house rules, much as she'd once done with Misty. Sometimes when her homework was finished, she would scoop Chloe into her arms and take her outside by the pool for fresh air and sunshine.

Since Chloe was primarily an indoor cat, the Boltons took him to the veterinarian to be declawed. After that, they were careful not to let him jump the fence around their home. Without his claws he would have no way to defend himself. Sometimes Tami lost track of Chloe and before she could stop her, the kitten would climb over the fence. But when that happened, the dogs on either side of the

Boltons' home would bark ferociously, and Tami would call Chloe back into her own yard.

Chloe developed a keen ear for Tami's voice and whenever she called her, the kitten would meow and scamper immediately back to her side.

"That's a good girl," Tami would say, cuddling Chloe close and rubbing her behind her ears.

There was no way to put into words how thankful Tami was for Chloe's presence in her life. Many times as Tami drifted off to sleep she would whisper a special thank-you to God for using the precious kitten to lift the dark cloud she'd been living under. Meanwhile, she kept in touch with Mari and learned that Misty was doing well.

Time was passing and Tami was surviving it. Her parents were right. One day they would finish up in California and they could go back home. Until then, Chloe was the best friend Tami could hope to have.

Then one day her warning system failed. One of the neighbors had taken their dog out for a walk, and by the time Tami realized what had happened, Chloe had disappeared. Frightened, Tami contacted both next-door neighbors and asked them to search their yards for the gray kitten. When neither found Chloe, Tami told herself that certainly the kitten would return within a few hours when she got hungry.

Five o'clock came, and then six. Still Chloe had not returned, and Tami was beginning to panic. Her parents arrived home, and together they searched the surrounding streets.

"Chloe, here kitty, kitty, kitty," Tami called as they walked. They searched for two hours, but there was no sign of the kitten.

Two days passed. Each afternoon Tami rushed back from her classes hoping to find her kitten home where she belonged. She walked up and down her neighborhood each afternoon asking neighbors if they'd seen her gray kitten and calling Chloe's name.

By the third afternoon, Tami began to lose hope. She walked home from the bus stop more slowly that day, a trickle of tears splashing on the ground near her tennis shoes. How could this happen? Why? She thought about God. *Lord, you let me find a friend and now you've let her disappear. Couldn't you bring Chloe back to me, God? Please.*

But the truth was clearer than Tami wanted to admit. The chances that Chloe would come back now—after so many days away—were almost nonexistent. Either something had happened to the kitty or she'd been taken by someone. Either way, Tami had to face the facts. She would probably never see Chloe again.

She set her books on the kitchen counter and went into the backyard.

"Chloe," she yelled as loud as she could. "Here, Chloe."

She stood waiting for a response, until finally her fear and loneliness overwhelmed her and she turned back toward the house, running into her bedroom. There, she threw herself on her bed and began yelling at God. She thought of a Bible verse in Lamentations that says, "Pour out your heart like water in the presence of the Lord."

And that was exactly what she did.

"God, I can't handle this! I'm so lonely and Chloe was all I had. Now she's gone, too!" Her sobs filled the room. "I just can't handle this. It's too much."

She continued for several minutes until her anger and frustration were spent. Then, still crying, she remembered another scripture, Psalms 34:18, which says, "The Lord is close to the brokenhearted and saves those who are crushed in spirit."

Suddenly, Tami felt God's presence, and in her grief she clung to the feeling. The chasm that had developed between her and God disappeared in an instant. *You're my friend, too, right God? Is that what you're trying to tell me?* A surge of hope welled up within her. Yes, that was it. God was her friend, now and always. A friend even better than Chloe.

No longer angry, she looked upward and whispered yet another prayer. "Please, Lord, hear me now. I only need you. But I really want my cat to come home, too." She thought a moment. "I'm going to go out into the backyard and I beg you to bring Chloe home for me. If it is your will, Lord, please answer my prayer."

Tami realized that her request sounded childish, but she trusted with all her heart that God could hear her. She walked down the hallway and opened the back door. There, sitting by the pool, was Chloe. She glanced at Tami casually as if she'd been there all the time.

"Meow," she squeaked. Then she scampered toward Tami.

Tami fell to her knees, bowing her head in thanks. Not because her cat was back home. But because she had rediscovered a different best friend. The sweetest friend of all.

Heaven's Perfect Timing

Her freshman year, Amy Baron commuted between college and home so often she became expert at it. She was just eighteen, younger than her peers at school and her parents wanted her to wait until the next fall before taking a dorm on campus. Amy agreed. She was the oldest of six kids and though the commute took an hour each way, she would miss her family too much to live at school.

"It's not an easy drive, honey," her father had told her when she started college. "Storms come up quickly around here. Please be careful. If it's bad weather, wait it out."

Time and again throughout the year, Amy found her father to be right. Especially during the winter, when storms could blow in with little or no warning. When that happened, roads became perilous and deaths on the area's highways were common. The most difficult part of Amy's commute was a stretch of roadway locals called, "The Summit," a particularly dangerous stretch with winding turns and steep drop-offs.

One day that January, Amy walked out of her last class and gazed at the sky. Menacing clouds were moving in along the eastern skyline. For a long moment, Amy stood still while other students made their way around her. She studied the clouds. Were they moving closer? Her eyes shifted to the blue sky above her and she whispered a prayer.

God . . . I have so much homework. Please help me get home safely. Keep the storm away, okay?

Then she hurried toward her car. But just as she opened the door a gust of wind blew across the parking lot. Amy looked skyward again and noticed that the air had grown very still. She shuddered. Her life had been filled with enough severe snowstorms to understand what the stillness meant. The storm was ready to bear down on anything in its path.

"Please, God..." This time she whispered the words out loud as she climbed inside. "Let me get through safely. Don't let me cross that Summit if it's going to be too dangerous."

She drove along surface streets toward Route 22, wondering if she should wait it out or try to cross the Summit before the storm hit. She could feel her stomach churning. Usually if the sky was blue, she'd take a chance and make it just fine. But something about these clouds looked more dangerous, more ominous, than usual. She knew she would have to drive up the steep grade of the Allegheny Mountains before reaching the Summit, where the roadway leveled out at the top of the mountain range. Route 22 was extremely dangerous there because without the protection of surrounding mountains crosswinds made driving treacherous even in mild weather. Signs warning drivers about the danger of crosswinds were scattered along the Summit. But still accidents were commonplace.

Amy continued making her way toward the on ramp, frustrated by the heavy traffic. There seemed to be a sense of panic and confusion among the other drivers as people flooded the roads, attempting to reach their destinations before the storm descended. Wind began blowing, and Amy was thankful that Route 22 was less than a block away.

Then, up ahead, she spotted a fast-food restaurant.

Suddenly she was gripped by a strong urge to pull in and order something from the drive-through window. She shook off the feeling, determined to stay on the road. Every minute would be crucial in clearing the Summit before the storm. The traffic crept forward, and again Amy was nearly overcome with the desire to pull off the road and get something to eat.

"This is crazy." She muttered the words out loud and tapped out a nervous beat on the steering wheel. It was two o'clock and she'd eaten lunch at school. There was no reason why she should be hungry. She drew a deep breath. She never stopped for food on the way home from college and today would not be an exception. Her family would have dinner in a few hours, after all.

But the more determined she was to wait until later to eat, the more persistent became the urge to stop. Now. As she drew closer to the fast-food restaurant, Amy's skin became hot and tingly and she felt light-headed. She exhaled hard and slumped in her seat. She was prone to bouts of low blood sugar, but usually only if she skipped a meal. Still, there was no question her symptoms were just that.

Can't I wait, Lord? Do I have to eat now? I want to get home so badly, God.

Just as she was about to pass the restaurant and proceed down the road, a voice rang through the car.

"Stop and eat, Amy."

Her eyes flew open and she shot a look at the backseat. There was no one there, no one else in the car. At the same time she checked the radio. But it was off. A chill ran down her arms. She had heard the voice as clearly as if someone was sitting beside her. But with even the radio off, there was no logical explanation as to where it came from. Stop and eat? Amy played the words over in her mind.

At the last possible instant, she stepped on the brake and turned into the fast-food restaurant parking lot toward the drive-through window.

Still baffled by the voice and her own actions, Amy ordered a cheeseburger and then waited.

She stared at the approaching clouds, her heart ricocheting strangely within her. The cashier seemed to take an eternity preparing and bagging her order.

"Come on, hurry." Amy leaned back against the headrest until finally her sandwich was ready. The sky was growing still darker, and she was terrified at what would happen if she didn't get on the highway soon.

Finally the cashier handed her the burger and Amy drove off. She was about to pull back into traffic when another wave of heat and clamminess washed over her. The feeling reminded her of a time when she'd broken her ankle and immediately afterwards fainted from the pain. But there was something different about the way she was feeling now. Almost as though the heat was emanating from somewhere inside her body. She saw an open parking spot and without thinking, she pulled her car into the spot and turned off the engine.

"Why am I wasting so much time?" She was angry with herself, frustrated at her indecision and the strange feelings that nearly suffocated her. "I've got to get on the road. Mom and Dad'll be scared to death about me."

Giving in, she loosened her coat and seat belt and ate the cheeseburger. Instantly she felt better, and in a moment the intense heat and clammy feeling were gone completely. Because she was prone to low blood sugar, there had been times when Amy had felt light-headed before. But never had eating caused those feelings to disappear so quickly.

Her strength renewed, Amy strapped her seat belt back into place and eased her car into traffic. Although the sky was frighteningly dark, there was still no snow, and she whispered a prayer of thanks as she drove up the on ramp for Route 22 and began climbing toward the Summit.

Minutes later, as her car continued to climb the mountainside, snowflakes hit her windshield. She drew a deep breath. *Okay, Amy . . . you can do it. Please God . . . guide me.* She flipped on the headlights and kept her eyes on the road ahead. Careful to leave a safe distance between her car and the one in front of her, she continued up the mountain.

As she drew closer to the Summit, the snow began coming down in sheets.

Fear wrapped its arms around her. She should have stayed back at the restaurant. Even if it meant waiting until the next day to go home, it would've been better than trying to cross the mountain range in a blinding snowstorm. Gripping the steering wheel tightly with both hands, Amy slowed some and continued up the road to the level place along the top of the Summit. Suddenly, without the protection of the mountain range, the snow completely engulfed the roadway. Amy was in the middle of a whiteout, with wind howling in different directions and huge snowflakes making it impossible to see more than a few feet.

Amy's heart beat wildly as she gently pumped the brakes. If someone hit her from behind, even a minor accident could send her through the guardrails, tumbling to certain death thousands of feet below. She fixed her eyes ahead, glancing occasionally into the rearview mirror. No matter how hard she tried, she couldn't make out anything but the front of her own car.

One minute passed, then two. Finally Amy saw that the car she was following had stopped. She could see only his taillights immediately in front of her and had no idea whether either of their cars were still on the highway. But at least she was no longer moving through the blinding snow, and when she saw lights stopping behind her as well, she allowed herself to feel relieved. *The traffic's stopped everywhere,* she thought. *We'll have to wait it out.*

Minutes passed and then abruptly, as quickly as it had settled over them, the snow cloud lifted and Amy could see that she was the tenth car behind a jackknifed tractor-trailer blocking the road. The driver was out of the cab walking around, and no other vehicles seemed to be involved.

"Thank God no one's hurt." Amy picked up her cell phone and dialed her parents' number.

"It's Amy. I got stuck in a snowstorm on the Summit."

"Honey, we've been worried sick." There was relief in her father's voice. "Is it safe now?"

"The storm's lifted. But there's a jack-knifed truck

in front of me. It could be awhile." Amy hesitated. "Daddy, I'm sorry. I should've waited until the storm passed."

"Is it still snowing?"

"No. It left as quickly as it came."

There was a pause on the other end. "Wait a minute." A news program sounded in the background. "Amy, there's an accident up there. Right where you are. Can you see it?"

Amy peered ahead of her. "All I can see is the truck. Doesn't look like any other cars are involved."

The traffic began to inch forward. "Be careful, honey. It's still dangerous until the roads are clear."

"I know. The roads must be a mess everywhere." Traffic continued to inch past the tractor-trailer, and Amy followed it. The moment she moved past the wreckage, she shrieked. "Dad...no! It's too awful!"

"What?" Her father's voice was filled with alarm. "Amy, are you there?"

"You can't believe what I'm seeing." Amy felt tears sting her eyes as she described the scene to her father. On the other side of the jackknifed truck there were dozens of cars smashed together, piled on top of each other in the ditch between the two sides of the highway.

It was easy to see what had happened.

When the whiteout came upon the Summit, the drivers must have done everything possible to avoid going over the cliffs. In doing so they had overcompensated and driven into the center ditch, hitting each other head-on in several cases.

"I have to stop, Dad. Someone might need my help."

"Amy..." Her father stopped himself and sighed. "Please be careful, sweetheart. Call me when you get back into the car."

Amy hung up and pulled her car over. The man in the car in front of her did the same and climbed out, running toward the mangled stretch of vehicles. Moments later he returned and asked Amy if he could use her cell phone.

"It's unbelievable." He pointed back to the mangled stretch of cars. "People are lying all over the road. Some of them look like they're dead." The man shook his head. His teeth chattered in the icy wind. "A few minutes earlier and we'd have been in that disaster. It makes you wonder, doesn't it?"

A sudden sense of knowing passed over Amy.

"Is there anything I can do?"

The man shook his head. "I'll call for help. These people need a lot more than you or I can do."

While he placed the call, something on the floorboard of her car caught Amy's eye. The crumpled empty cheeseburger wrapper! Suddenly it all made sense. If she hadn't heeded the voice, if she hadn't stopped and gotten something to eat, her car would be one of those caught in the massive accident. She might even be dead now.

Amy closed her eyes and remembered something

else. It had taken just seven minutes for her to pull off the road, purchase the burger, and eat it. Seven minutes. But God had used that precious bit of time to keep her from certain tragedy.

"Here you go." The man's voice interrupted her thoughts, and she opened her eyes. He handed her the phone. "They're sending a dozen ambulances." He turned to go. "I'm going to see if there's anything else I can do. You stay here. It's not something I'd want my daughter to see."

In minutes, ambulances arrived at the scene, and police ordered Amy and the other unharmed drivers in the area to remain in their cars as rescue vehicles raced to the accident victims. An hour later they were given permission to turn around and follow a police escort back down the highway, since the road was closed to all oncoming traffic.

It took nearly three hours for Amy to drive home using a detour route. During that time she pondered the importance of prayer and the mercy of God. She also prayed for the victims who had not been spared. Why had she been allowed to live? And why had others died? Amy swallowed hard and kept her eyes on the road. It was hard to imagine that God had been so merciful to her and yet had allowed many of the others to perish.

Then she remembered something her father had told her once. The kindest thing God had ever done was provide a way to heaven through Jesus Christ. Today simply wasn't her day to go home. And that was part of the mystery of God. He saw things differently, and only he knew the reasons why things had happened the way they did.

Weeks later, a white cross was erected at the site of that afternoon's horrific pileup on Route 22. Thirty vehicles had been involved in the accident, and nearly a dozen people had lost their lives. The cross was placed near one of the crucial signs warning of the perilously dangerous crosswinds that plague the Summit and the risk of sudden storms in the area.

Amy still commutes across the Summit to and from school, but she has moved into a dorm and makes the trip less often. Still, every time she does, she drives by a certain fast-food restaurant, whispers a heartfelt thank-you to God, and remembers the day he used a cheeseburger to save her life.

A Charlie Brown Christmas Miracle

Greg Jamison had always been the most popular guy at school. Though some of his buddies drank, he had always stayed away from alcohol. Until that fateful winter week during Christmas break.

Tall with dark hair and blue eyes, Greg was handsome and athletic. Every sport he played came easily to him. The trouble was it came *too* easily for him. Because of that he had stopped relying on God, stopped attending his parents' church, and almost stopped believing altogether.

That winter week, football season had ended and basketball hadn't yet begun. Greg had used the time to attend a handful of parties and do something he had always meant to avoid—drink beers with his buddies. At first the alcohol had burned his throat, but after a while it wasn't so bad. And the way he felt after a few drinks made talking to the girls even easier than usual.

After a week of drinking with his friends, staying

out late, and sleeping in until noon, one of his friends asked him to another party. But this time the stakes were higher.

"I scored some pot," his friend told him. "There's nothing like it, man. You gotta go."

"Alright, cool. See ya there." Greg's stomach churned the moment he heard himself say the words.

On the night of the party, he fought with his parents before leaving.

"You've been out too much this week, Greg." His mother caught up with him near the front door. "Stay home tonight. We're watching A *Charlie Brown Christmas*."

For a single moment, a twinge of regret pierced Greg's heart. Charlie Brown's Christmas special had once been his favorite holiday movie. But that was a lifetime ago. The moment passed as quickly as it had come and Greg made a face. "I'm too old for that. And I'm too old to stay home during Christmas break."

His father had entered the conversation then. "Watch your tone, Son. As long as you're living under our roof you need to show a little more respect."

Greg had uttered a few apologies and dashed out the door as quickly as he could. Now it was almost nine and he had spent the past hour driving the country roads near his Wichita, Kansas, home wondering what was happening to his life. Wasn't it just last year that he had promised himself and his parents he'd never get involved in the party scene the way his friends had? And what about the sports he was involved in? His coaches wouldn't want him if he got into drinking and drugs. And coaches knew about those types of things. If the basketball coaches got wind of what he'd been doing over Christmas break, they could cut him from the team.

And what about God? Where did he fit in this picture? If there was a God—and his parents sure believed there was—then Greg was bound to be in big trouble. Because God would probably kick him out of the family for doing drugs that past week. But what if there was no God? What if you only lived your life and then died with no existence, no heaven or hell?

The possibilities swirled through Greg's mind, leaving him too confused to think straight. He leaned back against the headrest and drew in a slow breath. Why was he worrying about tomorrow, anyway? The party was probably in full swing by now. At least if he went there, he could forget about the huge questions banging around in his head. A few drugs wouldn't hurt him, would they? And besides, he wouldn't have to think about his future, at least until the morning.

The longer Greg thought about his situation, the more convinced he became that he should go to the party. "A *Charlie Brown Christmas*..." He muttered the words out loud. "Like I'd wanna watch that when I could be out with my friends."

He was about to turn around and head toward the party when suddenly he spotted what looked like a prison guard hitchhiking along the side of the road. Greg had never picked up a hitchhiker, but something about the man suggested he was on the way to work and genuinely in need of a ride. The prison was about ten miles down the road, so it made sense. Maybe the guy's car had broken down.

Greg pulled over and rolled down his window. The man stooped down and looked inside. His eyes were a kind, gentle brown and his smile looked harmless.

"Need a ride?"

The guard nodded. "Thanks. I was hoping you'd stop." His words were slow and carefully measured. "Car's broken down."

"You work at the prison?" Greg motioned down the road. In the recesses of his mind he questioned what he was about to do. His parents had always told him not to pick up hitchhikers. But there was something trustworthy about the man—something Greg couldn't quite figure out.

"Yep." The guard angled his head so he could see Greg better. "My shift starts in five minutes."

"Get in." Greg unlocked the door. He hadn't seen any broken-down cars alongside the roadway, but the man seemed kind enough. Greg was not afraid that his hitchhiking might be some kind of ruse to rob or harm him.

As the man climbed inside, Greg glanced over

and saw he was well into his fifties, with graying hair and a moustache. Somehow his face had a glow about it, even in the dark of night. His prison guard uniform was perfectly pressed, and he seemed strangely out of place in it.

"What's your name?" Greg picked up speed and headed toward the prison.

"Ralph. Ralph Michaels. Worked at the prison for the past ten years."

Greg was silent a moment. The man beside him seemed unusually calm and relaxed, considering he was late for work and traveling with a stranger in an unfamiliar car after a breakdown of his own.

After nearly a minute, the prison guard turned toward him, and again his face was full of light. "Now, why don't you tell me what's on your mind?"

Greg was unsure what to make of the man, but he shrugged and started telling him his age and what he was studying in school.

"No," the man said softly. "Tell me about the crossroad."

Greg stared at the man, wondering how he could have known to ask such a question. "What do you mean?"

"You know what I mean. You have some choices you're trying to make, don't you?"

Greg felt strangely uncomfortable, as if the man could somehow read his thoughts. But he shrugged once again, convincing himself that the man could not possibly have known anything about his personal life. The stranger was only lonely and looking for conversation.

Still, Greg felt like talking. With a loud sigh, he began to tell the man the truth. He told him about his upbringing and how his parents prayed for him daily.

"But I'm different now; that kind of life is in my past." Greg waved his hand, his tone filled with frustration.

"No." The man's voice was sudden and firm. Greg looked at him; he was shaking his head. "That kind of life is closer than you think."

"You're a prison guard. What would you know?" Greg was suddenly irritated. His beliefs were none of this man's business.

"I do know." The man's answer was not defensive or angry, but he spoke with a finality that set Greg on edge.

"Look…I don't know who you are, but yeah, okay. I'm at a crossroads. I've been good all my life and now I want to find some things out for myself." Greg peered over at the man. "Know what I mean?"

The man said nothing. He stared straight ahead for several minutes before turning again toward Greg. "There's only one right way. You know that, right?"

"Look, I'm tired of talking." The prison had just appeared on their right, and Greg pulled over. His tone was abrupt but he didn't care. He had a party to get to. "Where can I drop you off?"

The man smiled, his attitude unchanged by Greg's rudeness. "This is fine." He turned toward Greg once more. "Make the right choice, son. Now. You still have the chance, you know." He climbed out, shut the door and paused. "Besides . . . A *Charlie Brown Christmas* isn't so bad, is it, Greg?"

"No—" A strange sense of awe and wonder gripped Greg's heart. "No, it isn't."

The man winked. "I didn't think so." Then he turned and headed up the long driveway toward the prison.

As Greg pulled away he was stunned by the encounter with the man. How had an old prison guard known his name? Greg couldn't remember ever saying it. Or telling him about the Charlie Brown special. For a moment Greg wanted to turn around and follow the guy, spend more time talking with him and glean something from the wisdom he seemed to possess. But the night was late and suddenly he wanted nothing more than to go back home. If he was lucky, maybe his parents hadn't started the Charlie Brown movie yet.

Through the night and into the next morning Greg thought over everything the man had said. How had he known so much? And why would he have been hitchhiking to work when he lived so far from the prison? There was something else, too. A sense of relief stronger than his need for air. Because of the prison guard, Greg had avoided going to the party and taking drugs. In fact, the entire party scene looked suddenly dangerous and, well, crazy, really.

All because of a few minutes with a stranger.

Finally Greg decided he needed to talk to the man once more. He called the prison from his bedroom later that afternoon. "I'd like to speak to Ralph Michaels. He's a prison guard." Greg wondered what exactly he would say to the man, how he could explain the changes in his heart in the past few hours.

"Hmmm." There was a pause on the other end. "I don't believe he works here."

Greg furrowed his eyebrows. "Of course he works there. He was going to work last night and I gave him a ride. He had his uniform on."

"Well, I can let you talk with my supervisor, but I've got the employee list right here. There isn't any prison guard named Ralph Michaels at this facility."

"Fine." Greg could feel his frustration rising. "Let me talk to your supervisor."

The supervisor spent ten minutes convincing Greg that there wasn't now and never had been a Ralph Michaels employed at the prison. Greg described the man and the place where he'd dropped him off outside the prison. "Maybe he works under a different name."

Again the supervisor was quick to disagree. "The guys working last night were in their twenties. There was no one on duty like the man you're describing.

Besides, we have background checks—we wouldn't let anyone work under an assumed name."

At Greg's request, she also checked the other prison facilities in the state, but none of them employed a Ralph Michaels either.

Stunned, Greg hung up the phone. The man had ridden with him for ten minutes, giving him subtle advice about his life and trying to point him in the right direction. Now he had disappeared, almost as if he had never existed.

Later that night, Greg told his parents about the experience.

"Sometimes God gets our attention in interesting ways." His mother's voice was quiet and kind. "Did you ever think that he might have been an angel?"

"An angel? Like in the Bible stories?" Greg felt his heartbeat double.

"Why not? God is still God, and his ways aren't so different now than they were back in Bible times."

For several weeks Greg considered the possibility, until finally he was convinced that his mother was right. Ralph must have been an angel sent to guide him through a time in his life when he had crucial choices to make. How better for God to get his attention than with a prison guard, especially in light of the choices he'd been making up until that point.

Almost overnight, Greg decided he would no longer involve himself in drinking or all-night parties.

Instead, over the next year he doubled his efforts toward school and sports and began attending church again. He found a peace and assurance he had never believed could exist. Eventually Greg earned a degree in telecommunications and went on to serve as a reporter for one of the television news shows in southern Florida.

One of his first feature assignments? "Angels among us—true stories of God's miraculous presence today."

Invisible Protection

For the first time ever, Mia Parsons and her friend Tanya Andrews were going to spend New Year's Eve with a hundred thousand people in downtown Pasadena, California. Excitement didn't come close to describing the way they felt. It was the chance of a lifetime, proof that they were finally growing up.

Never, not once, did either girl think the trip could cost them their lives.

In fact, they were seventeen that year and thrilled that they were old enough to celebrate New Year's Eve at the all-night party preceding the annual Tournament of Roses Parade along the streets of Pasadena. When morning came, the two friends would watch the parade and then return home.

The girls and their parents believed the plan was both simple and safe. They would travel together in Mia's car and set up alongside a dozen other friends who would also be lined along the parade route. The girls didn't drink and would easily avoid the alcohol-induced revelry that would be going on around them. Besides, their group of friends were good kids, part of their high school's local Young Life club. They'd have plenty of fun without drinking.

Mia was not concerned about the party-types who would surround them on the parade route. Her only hesitation was Tanya. The girl was a new friend and had only been attending Young Life for a few weeks. Mia wasn't completely sure how crazy Tanya might get out on the parade route. But whatever happened, she intended to set the pace. That way Tanya would know her limits. And regardless of how crazy things might get around them, Mia did not foresee any problems.

At first the night went as planned. She and Tanya met up with their Young Life friends and found a place along the parade route. The group laughed and danced to the music that filled the street from all directions. Despite the darkness, crowds of people walked along the parade route dressed in flamboyant attire, waving flags and shouting greetings of "Happy New Year!" Others openly tilted champagne bottles and beer cans while hooting in preparation for the approaching midnight hour.

Although Mia and her group would not be drinking that night, they had met some teens on a blanket beside their group who would be. She silently hoped none of them would get sick or hurt. The thought passed quickly and Mia began enjoying herself and the mood of the celebration around her.

About that time a small man walked past Mia and her group of friends. Abruptly he turned, set his eyes on Mia, and slowly approached her. As he reached her, he handed her a yellow sticker that read "Jesus loves you."

"Thanks." Mia smiled as she took the sticker. "He loves you, too."

The man nodded and gave Mia a calm smile. Then he turned away and proceeded down Colorado Boulevard.

"That was strange." Mia pulled Tanya aside.

"What?" Tanya looked around, confused.

"That man I was talking to." Mia pointed to the sticker on the sleeve of her shirt. "He just walked up and gave me this."

Tanya shrugged. "It's New Year's Eve. You never know who you'll meet down here tonight."

"Yeah, I guess." Mia gazed down the street, but the man was no longer in sight. She smiled. "At least it's true. The sticker, I mean."

"Enough about the sticker." Tanya grabbed Mia's sleeve. "Come on. Everyone's waiting for us."

As the girls returned to their group of friends, Mia dismissed her thoughts of the man. The evening progressed, and people began cruising

Colorado Boulevard in their cars, greeting those lined along the parade route and lending their music to the party before moving slowly along the street. Mia and her friends joined in the fun, waving to the people in the cars. It was more fun than Mia had dared to hope and she could hardly wait for midnight.

An hour later, the cars lined up along the boulevard were bumper to bumper and barely moving. At about that time, a pickup truck with two good-looking young men pulled up in front of the girls.

"Wanna ride?" one of them called out.

Mia stifled a laugh. "Right!" she shouted over the roar of noise that filled the street. "Like we'd take a ride with a total stranger."

The young man smiled. "Oh, come on. We're just circling the parade route. Climb in back. We'll take you around once and drop you back off."

Mia and Tanya exchanged a knowing glance, silently agreeing that the driver was indeed very handsome. At that instant, Steve Simons from their Young Life group stepped in. "What's going on?"

Mia pointed to the guy in the truck. She was grateful for the protection of the group. "He wants to take us around the route once."

Steve looked from the guy in the truck to Mia and Tanya. "Do you know him?"

"Yes." Tanya stepped forward. "From school." She shot a desperate look at Mia. "Right?"

Mia eyed the truck and the handsome boys inside. What harm could come if she and Tanya sat in the back and rode once around the parade route? Traffic was moving so slowly that they could always jump out if they didn't want to stay with the guys.

A smile lifted the corners of her lips. "Sure." She grinned at Tanya. "We met 'em last year."

"Well?" The driver of the truck smiled, his eyes shining. Behind him cars were backed up and honking at him. "You coming or not?"

Mia looked at Tanya and shrugged. What could it hurt? Besides, it was New Year's Eve. Grabbing her friend's hand, Mia pulled her toward the truck. "Sure. You only live once. Let's go!"

Steve Simons stepped back. "As long as you know them," he shouted as they pulled away. "Be careful."

Tanya and Mia situated themselves against the rear of the cab and waved at the thousands of people lined up on either side of the road. The wind felt wonderful on Mia's face and her heart was light within her. So what if they'd told Steve a small lie. This was the life, wasn't it? Riding along with a couple of gorgeous guys, celebrating the New Year in style.

For twenty minutes the fun continued. Mia and Tanya laughed and sang songs at the top of their lungs. They linked arms and pretended it was New Year's morning and they were part of the parade.

A few times the guys yelled something out the side windows, and always their tone sounded happy and upbeat.

But when thirty minutes had passed, Mia suddenly noticed that the crowd lining the street had thinned. There were no longer markers indicating that they were on the parade route. At about that time she spun around and stared at the guys in the cab. The driver leaned over and whispered something to his friend, and both laughed out loud.

That's when Mia noticed that both guys were drinking. There were several empty beer cans along the floor of their vehicle.

Just then the vehicle came to a stop at an intersection. "We're leaving Pasadena!" She gripped Tanya's arm. "The guys are leaving with us!"

Suddenly, above the noise of the boys' truck radio, Mia heard a voice whisper in her ear, "Get out! They're taking you to the beach to rape you."

Panic filled Mia's heart. She had no time to wonder who had whispered the warning as she peered through the back window and the windshield. What she saw made her heart skip a beat. They were about to enter the westbound Ventura Freeway—a route that eventually would lead them to the beach.

"Quick!" she shouted at Tanya. "We're in trouble! Get out!" Tanya's mouth fell open but she made no move to jump out of the truck.

Just then, the driver sped up so that they were

moving twice as fast as before. Mia gasped. He must have heard her scream and now he was barreling toward the freeway ramp.

In a split-second decision Mia knew she would rather die on a roadway in Pasadena than be taken to the beach and raped. *God? I've gotten myself in a crazy spot here. Help me . . . please!* She crawled toward the back of the truck, stood up, and jumped onto the roadway before Tanya could stop her.

Mia felt herself sail through the air. *This is it,* she thought, *I'm going to die and I'll never have the chance to tell my parents I'm sorry.* Then there was nothing but silence.

Cars from all directions came to a screeching halt as Mia's body slammed onto the pavement and slid into the middle of the intersection. Although a number of cars were traveling fast and headed right toward her, one at a time each of them swerved and missed hitting her.

Later, one of the passersby would say there seemed almost to be a protective shield around the girl as she lay in the road untouched by the heavy traffic. A motorcycle police officer had seen what happened. He called for help and was instantly at Mia's side. He had worked enough accident scenes to know that the girl would have serious injuries. Perhaps even fatal injuries.

He ran to her side. "Don't move." He reached for her pulse. "I've already called for help."

Mia couldn't make sense of what was happening.

She should've been terribly injured, but nothing hurt. Instead there was a strange sense of assurance, mingled with the greatest urgency she'd ever felt. "My friend!" Tears streamed down her face. "They're going to rape my friend."

The officer looked up and saw the pickup truck. For a moment, the truck had temporarily pulled off to the side of the road when Mia had jumped. But now the driver was attempting to enter the freeway once again. Immediately the officer climbed back onto his motorcycle, flipped on his red lights, and in a few seconds pulled the truck over.

As soon as the truck stopped, Tanya climbed out the back and ran toward Mia, who was still in the middle of the street. Several drivers and parade goers had rushed to the scene and were gathered around her, trying to help. Tanya was crying when she reached her friend.

"Why did you do that, Mia?" She stood over her friend and ran her hand through her hair. "You could have killed yourself!"

"They were going to rape us, Tanya. I heard it. Someone told me they were going to take us to the beach and rape us."

Tanya's face grew pale. "Who said it? I didn't hear anything."

Mia pointed toward the freeway signs. "Look. They left the parade route a long time ago, and they were just about to take us on the freeway. They're drinking, Tanya. As soon as we got on the freeway, we would have been good as dead. Don't you see?"

Tanya looked back at the truck where the police officer was administering a sobriety test to the young man behind the wheel. "Mia, you're right. I can't believe we were so stupid." Tanya was terrified as she knelt by her friend's side. "Are you okay?"

For the first time since jumping from the car, Mia rolled onto her back and sat up. She was wearing long white denim jeans and her eyes grew wide as she ran her fingers over her knees. She had fallen right onto the pavement and skidded several feet along the asphalt before coming to a stop. Yet the knees and fronts of her jeans were completely clean and unharmed.

Suddenly Mia remembered that as she hit the road she had seemed to lose all sense of feeling in her body. There had been no pain, no fear—only a certainty that she had done what she had to do to save her life.

Now as she remembered the strange sensation of landing on the road without pain, she looked at the palms of her hands. She had seen her hands sliding along the street and knew they should have been torn apart from the rough road. But as she examined them she found that they, too, were unharmed. Her skin was as soft and unscratched as if she had never touched the road.

"I'm fine," she whispered. "Can you see this, Tanya? I'm *perfectly* fine."

Tanya studied her friend and for a long while she said nothing. She had seen the way Mia had jumped from the car and landed harshly on the pavement. It was impossible that she would be unmarked by the fall.

Mia stood up and looked herself over once more. There wasn't even any dirt to brush off her body, and she felt perfectly fine. Too stunned to wait for the police officer, she motioned for Tanya to follow her, and the girls set off walking back toward their friends. They were silent much of the way, until at last their group came into sight. At that moment Mia stopped and glanced down at her shirtsleeve. There was the sticker, also completely unscathed by the jump.

"Jesus loves me," she said out loud, her voice almost trancelike. Then she looked at Tanya. "What just happened doesn't make sense. I jumped from a moving truck and I'm perfectly fine." She paused for what seemed like nearly a minute. "Tanya," she finally said, taking the sticker from her sleeve and holding it carefully in her hand. "It was a miracle what happened tonight. That's why that man gave me this sticker. I think God knew what was going to happen, and he looked out for us."

Tanya reached out and hugged her friend tightly. It was obvious that it would be a long time before the shock of what had happened that night would wear off. "How come you're not cut up or hurt?"

Tanya walked in a slow circle around Mia. "I mean, you don't have a scratch on you!"

"I know...thank God." Mia felt the sting of tears in her eyes. "It'll be a New Year's Eve I'll never forget."

Now It's Your Turn . . .

You've had the chance to sort through A *Treasury of Miracles for Teens* and allow the stories to touch your heart. Now it's your turn. The following section of blank pages is offered here for you, as a way for you to include your story among this treasury.

Some of you are nodding and reaching for a pen. The idea of writing the story of something special God has done for you is an easy one. But others of you are shaking your head, not certain you actually have a story. For you, I offer the following questions to jump-start your memory.

- Have you ever had a super serious prayer request or need and then everything somehow worked out? If so, the problem, prayer, and solution is a story waiting to be written.
- Have you ever witnessed something amazing or miraculous where one of your friends or family

members was concerned? If so, this miracle story is worth putting down on paper.

- Was there ever a time when a stranger offered you help, hope, or encouragement? Is it possible that person could have been an angel? Write the story and be careful to include the little details.
- Have you or any of your friends or family experienced an increase in faith, and in the process witnessed a miraculous change in some aspect of life? Tell about the before and after of this person, and again, look for the amazing details that make a difference.

Remember, this collection isn't complete until it has your story here in the back of the book. It's a treasury—a treasure chest of stories—and nothing could be more precious than your personal account of God's miraculous presence among us.

Grab your pen and get writing. This will be a book you'll want to keep around. That way, when the news shouting at you from the TV is nothing but bad, you'll have something to fall back on.

And better yet, a reason to believe.

#1 *New York Times* Author
Karen Kingsbury

STANDALONE TITLES
Between Sundays
The Bridge
The Chance
Coming Home, the Baxter Family
Divine
Fifteen Minutes
Like Dandelion Dust
Oceans Apart
On Every Side
Shades of Blue
This Side of Heaven (with friends from Cody Gunner series)
Unlocked
When Joy Came to Stay
Where Yesterday Lives

E-SHORTS
The Beginning
I Can Only Imagine

REDEMPTION SERIES—BAXTERS 1
Redemption—*Book 1*
Remember—*Book 2*
Return—*Book 3*
Rejoice—*Book 4*
Reunion—*Book 5*

FIRSTBORN SERIES—BAXTERS 2
Fame—*Book 1*
Forgiven—*Book 2*
Found—*Book 3*
Family—*Book 4*
Forever—*Book 5*

Sunrise Series—Baxters 3

Sunrise—Book 1

Summer—Book 2

Someday—Book 3

Sunset—Book 4

Above the Line Series—Baxters 4

Take One—Book 1

Take Two—Book 2

Take Three—Book 3

Take Four—Book 4

Bailey Flanigan Series—Baxters 5

Leaving—Book 1

Learning—Book 2

Longing—Book 3

Loving—Book 4

Lost Love Series

Even Now—Book 1

Ever After—Book 2

September 11th Series

One Tuesday Morning—Book 1

Beyond Tuesday Morning—Book 2

Remember Tuesday Morning—Book 3

Timeless Love Series

A Time to Dance—Book 1

A Time to Embrace—Book 2

Cody Gunner Series

A Thousand Tomorrows—Book 1

Just Beyond the Clouds—Book 2

Forever Faithful Series

Waiting for Morning—Book 1

Moment of Weakness—Book 2

Halfway to Forever—Book 3

Red Glove Titles

Gideon's Gift

Maggie's Miracle

Sarah's Song

Hannah's Hope

Treasury of Miracles Books

A Treasury of Christmas Miracles

A Treasury of Miracles for Women

A Treasury of Miracles for Teens

A Treasury of Miracles for Friends

A Treasury of Adoption Miracles

Miracles Devotional

Children's Books

Always Daddy's Princess

For Flutterby

The Brave Young Knight

The Princess and the Three Knights

Let Me Hold You Longer

We Believe in Christmas

Let's Go on a Mommy Date

Let's Have a Daddy Day

Gift Books

Forever Young

Be Safe Little Boy

Stay Close Little Girl

www.KarenKingsbury.com